Neal Starkman

# Walking Your Talk

## Building Assets in Organizations That Serve Youth

Search INSTITUTE | *Practical research benefiting children and youth*

**Walking Your Talk: Building Assets in Organizations That Serve Youth**
Neal Starkman
Copyright © 2002 by Search Institute

At the time of this book's publication, all facts and figures cited are the most current available; all telephone numbers, addresses, and Web site URLs are accurate and active; all publications, organizations, Web sites, and other resources exist as described in this book; and all efforts have been made to verify them. The author and Search Institute make no warranty or guarantee concerning the information and materials given out by organizations or content found at Web sites, and we are not responsible for any changes that occur after this book's publication. If you find an error or believe that a resource listed here is not as described, please contact Client Services at Search Institute. We strongly urge you to monitor young people's use of the Internet.

10     9     8     7     6     5     4     3     2     1

Search Institute
615 First Avenue Northeast, Suite 125
Minneapolis, MN 55413
612-376-8955
800-888-7828
www.search-institute.org

**Credits**
Editor: Jennifer Griffin-Wiesner
Designer: Diane Gleba Hall
Production manager: Rebecca Manfredini

**Library of Congress Cataloging-in-Publication Data**
Starkman, Neal.
    Walking your talk : building assets in organizations that serve youth / Neal Starkman.
      p. cm.
    Includes bibliographical references.
    ISBN 1-57482-826-6
    1. Youth—Services for.  2. Youth—Societies and clubs.  3. Organizational effectiveness.  4. Developmental psychology.  5. Intergenerational relations. 6. Mentoring.  7. Social work with youth.  I. Search Institute (Minneapolis, Minn.) II.Title.

HV1421.S73 2002
362.7—dc21                                                    2002009079

## About Search Institute

Search Institute is an independent, nonprofit, nonsectarian organization whose mission is to advance the well-being of children and youth by generating knowledge and promoting its application. The institute collaborates with others to promote long-term organizational and cultural change that supports its mission.

Search Institute's Healthy Communities • Healthy Youth initiative seeks to motivate and equip individuals, organizations, and their leaders to join together in nurturing competent, caring, and responsible children and adolescents. The founding national sponsor for Healthy Communities • Healthy Youth is Thrivent Financial for Lutherans, a not-for-profit fraternal benefit society providing financial services and community service opportunities for Lutherans nationwide.

# Contents

# Figures

# Acknowledgments

Obviously, when one writes a book like this, one owes virtually everything to the people featured in it, the people who selflessly gave their time, their knowledge, and their materials so that you, the reader, could benefit. I want to mention in particular two remarkable individuals: Tommy Tinajero and William Powers. Each of them really went out of his way to host me, yet made it seem otherwise.

I also offer thanks to Jennifer Griffin-Wiesner, the editor of this book, whose ideas for reorganizing the chapters and other suggestions have, I trust, made this a much better resource.

Finally, a great deal of gratitude must be paid to you, the reader. I can write from now till the gazillionth of October, but you, collectively, are the ones who will make all this work.

*"We ought to be building a future with our youth."*

PAUL VIDAS, director, United with Youth, Menasha, Wisconsin

# 1
# Your Book

## Missions

*"To make a positive difference in the lives of children and youth."*
—BIG BROTHERS BIG SISTERS OF AMERICA

*"To inspire and enable all young people . . . to realize their full potential
as productive, responsible, and caring citizens."*
—BOYS AND GIRLS CLUBS OF AMERICA

*"To build caring, confident youth and future leaders."*
—CAMP FIRE USA

*"To develop self-potential."*
—GIRL SCOUTS

*"To build a world in which youth and adults learn, grow,
and work together as catalysts for positive change."*
—4-H

*"To build healthy spirit, mind, and body."*

—YMCA

*"To empower women and girls and to eliminate racism."*

—YWCA

Worthwhile missions all. Having missions like these is one reason why the organizations listed above are building developmental assets with the young people they serve.

While several large organizations—including the YMCAs of the USA and Canada and Camp Fire USA—have made national-level commitments to build developmental assets, some local affiliates of these and other organizations are also doing so even without knowing about developmental assets. Others have recently become aware of the asset framework and have found in it a new language to assess, plan, and talk about what they've been doing for years. And still others are beginning to build developmental assets intentionally and explicitly. What you'll learn in this book is how any organization that serves young people can serve them better by helping them build developmental assets.

*Walking Your Talk: Building Assets in Organizations That Serve Youth* is intended to help you move beyond spreading the word about the asset framework, as important as that is, to *actually building assets with young people.* More specifically, if you're associated in any way with an organization that serves youth, then this book is about walking *your* talk.

I've drawn here on my experiences over the past 30-some years developing curricula and training materials. I've specialized in innovative health education, particularly in the areas of drug education, HIV/AIDS prevention, violence prevention, and peer helping. More important, though, I draw here on the experiences of the 100 or so youth work professionals who took the time to talk and in some cases meet with me. Many also generously shared materials—forms, flyers, worksheets, surveys, descriptions of activities—that they've used to infuse assets into their organizations. I've titled this opening chapter "Your Book" because I'd like you not only to read these materials but also to *use* them: Copy them. Adapt them. Fax and e-mail them to people you think will use them. Strategies for building developmental assets shouldn't be secrets;

the idea is to make these strategies available. Your role is to use what you can and pass everything on.

In this first chapter you'll learn about developmental assets and what they might mean in terms of your attitudes and behavior toward young people. In Chapter 2, "Walking Relationships," I summarize what young people have told me they want from organizations and individuals that hope and intend to serve them—and serve them well. I also address "changing the rules" for adult-youth interactions. And you'll see how the idea of mentoring has redefined the relationships between adults and young people in organizations.

Chapter 3, "Walking Environments," describes the effort to build assets on an organizational level, a complex effort that often requires systemic, normative change. The chapter begins with an emphasis on the importance of empowering young people to thoroughly engage in organizational activities, and describes what some of those activities might be. In then examining how the asset framework can help organizations that serve youth plan their efforts more intentionally, I take you first through the initial vision of an organization, then to the mission and philosophy, and then to how that philosophy is translated into goals and implemented. I point out the importance of staffing in your organization and of monitoring everyone's efforts.

In Chapter 4, "Walking Programs and Activities," you'll get an idea of the kinds of things that young people are doing to build assets. You'll see how several organizations have extended themselves to form partnerships with other community organizations and with families in the pursuit of building assets. In the very important Chapter 5, "Walking You," I'll give you tools to help you build assets with young people. Chapter 5 is followed by questions that you might ask yourself to see where you are along the road to building assets. These are the same questions that you'll find in the margins throughout the book. And the final section, "Walkers," acknowledges and gives access to the people who contributed to the writing of this book and who continually contribute to building assets with young people.

*Walking Your Talk* has a mission, just as organizations that serve youth have missions. Our mission is not merely to help you tell people about assets and the asset framework, but to help you build assets, to build a future, as Paul Vidas says, *with* youth. Many people with whom

*What is your personal mission?*

*What is your organization's mission?*

*Are you committed to making a positive difference in the lives of young people?*

*What, specifically, are you committed to doing?*

the asset framework resonates are looking for ways to apply the framework to their work and personal lives. That's what this book is all about—action, commitment, and dedication. And if you're reading this book, then I'm guessing that's what you're all about, too.

## Developmental Assets

*"Developmental assets are what our program has always been about."*

—BETH MOWRY, director of membership, Girl Scouts—
Great Valley Council, Allentown, Pennsylvania

What are developmental assets? Search Institute—which pioneered the work on assets—often calls them "building blocks." They're positive relationships, experiences, values, attitudes, and attributes that contribute to healthy personal growth. Search Institute has identified 40 of them in the literature on human development and separated them into "external assets," which are structures, relationships, and activities that create a positive environment for young people, and "internal assets," which are values, skills, and beliefs that young people need in order to fully engage with and function in the world around them. The 40 developmental assets are listed in English and Spanish in Figures 1.1 and 1.2. Look them over. If you haven't seen them before, think about which ones you experienced when you were growing up—and which ones you did not.

The developmental assets all have one characteristic in common: They're associated with young people's success. The more of these assets young people experience, the likelier they are not only to succeed in school but also to avoid high-risk behaviors such as drug use, violence, and early sexual activity, as shown in Figure 1.3.

So, let's agree on a first, critical point: **Having assets is a good thing.**

Now, if you've never seen these assets before, your first thought may be that this isn't a big revelation. After all, who would argue that it's not good to have self-esteem or to believe that your community values you? Well, you're right; this isn't a big revelation, and therein lies one of the strengths of the developmental assets framework. It's common sense, so many people understand it almost immediately. They may not realize right away how it translates into their own behavior, and they may not necessarily see the implications of treating youth as resources, but they understand the principle. Your second thought may be that you feel

**Figure 1.1**

# 40 Developmental Assets

The framework of developmental assets identifies crucial relationships, experiences, opportunities, and personal qualities that children and adolescents need to grow up healthy, caring, and responsible.

...................................................................................................................

| Category | Asset Name and Definition |

...................................................................................................................

EXTERNAL ASSETS

...................................................................................................................

**Support**
1. **Family support**—Family life provides high levels of love and support.
2. **Positive family communication**—Young person and her or his parent(s) communicate positively, and young person is willing to seek advice and counsel from parent(s).
3. **Other adult relationships**—Young person receives support from three or more nonparent adults.
4. **Caring neighborhood**—Young person experiences caring neighbors.
5. **Caring school climate**—School provides a caring, encouraging environment.
6. **Parent involvement in schooling**—Parent(s) are actively involved in helping young person succeed in school.

...................................................................................................................

**Empowerment**
7. **Community values youth**—Young person perceives that adults in the community value youth.
8. **Youth as resources**—Young people are given useful roles in the community.
9. **Service to others**—Young person serves in the community one hour or more per week.
10. **Safety**—Young person feels safe at home, at school, and in the neighborhood.

...................................................................................................................

**Boundaries and Expectations**
11. **Family boundaries**—Family has clear rules and consequences, and monitors the young person's whereabouts.
12. **School boundaries**—School provides clear rules and consequences.
13. **Neighborhood boundaries**—Neighbors take responsibility for monitoring young people's behavior.
14. **Adult role models**—Parent(s) and other adults model positive, responsible behavior.
15. **Positive peer influence**—Young person's best friends model responsible behavior.
16. **High expectations**—Both parent(s) and teachers encourage the young person to do well.

...................................................................................................................

**Constructive Use of Time**
17. **Creative activities**—Young person spends three or more hours per week in lessons or practice in music, theater, or other arts.
18. **Youth programs**—Young person spends three or more hours per week in sports, clubs, or organizations at school and/or in the community.

| Category | Asset Name and Definition |
|---|---|

19. **Religious community**—Young person spends one or more hours per week in activities in a religious institution.
20. **Time at home**—Young person is out with friends "with nothing special to do" two or fewer nights per week.

## INTERNAL ASSETS

**Commitment to Learning**

21. **Achievement motivation**—Young person is motivated to do well in school.
22. **School engagement**—Young person is actively engaged in learning.
23. **Homework**—Young person reports doing at least one hour of homework every school day.
24. **Bonding to school**—Young person cares about her or his school.
25. **Reading for pleasure**—Young person reads for pleasure three or more hours per week.

**Positive Values**

26. **Caring**—Young person places high value on helping other people.
27. **Equality and social justice**—Young person places high value on promoting equality and reducing hunger and poverty.
28. **Integrity**—Young person acts on convictions and stands up for her or his beliefs.
29. **Honesty**—Young person "tells the truth even when it is not easy."
30. **Responsibility**—Young person accepts and takes personal responsibility.
31. **Restraint**—Young person believes it is important not to be sexually active or to use alcohol or other drugs.

**Social Competencies**

32. **Planning and decision making**—Young person knows how to plan ahead and make choices.
33. **Interpersonal competence**—Young person has empathy, sensitivity, and friendship skills.
34. **Cultural competence**—Young person has knowledge of and comfort with people of different cultural/racial/ethnic backgrounds.
35. **Resistance skills**—Young person can resist negative peer pressure and dangerous situations.
36. **Peaceful conflict resolution**—Young person seeks to resolve conflict nonviolently.

**Positive Identity**

37. **Personal power**—Young person feels he or she has control over "things that happen to me."
38. **Self-esteem**—Young person reports having a high self-esteem.
39. **Sense of purpose**—Young person reports that "my life has a purpose."
40. **Positive view of personal future**—Young person is optimistic about her or his personal future.

Figure 1.2

# 40 elementos fundamentales del desarrollo

La investigación realizada por el Instituto Search ha identificado los siguientes elementos fundamentales del desarrollo como instrumentos para ayudar a los jóvenes a crecer sanos, interesados en el bienestar común y a ser responsables.

## ELEMENTOS FUNDAMENTALES EXTERNOS

**Apoyo**

1. **Apoyo familiar**—La vida familiar brinda altos niveles de amor y apoyo.
2. **Comunicación familiar positiva**—El (La) joven y sus padres se comunican positivamente. Los jóvenes están dispuestos a buscar consejo y consuelo en sus padres.
3. **Otras relaciones con adultos**—Además de sus padres, los jóvenes reciben apoyo de tres o más personas adultas que no son sus parientes.
4. **Una comunidad comprometida**—El (La) joven experimenta el interés de sus vecinos por su bienestar.
5. **Un plantel educativo que se interesa por el (la) joven**—La escuela proporciona un ambiente que anima y se preocupa por la juventud.
6. **La participación de los padres en las actividades escolares**—Los padres participan activamente ayudando a los jóvenes a tener éxito en la escuela.

**Fortalecimiento**

7. **La comunidad valora a la juventud**—El (La) joven percibe que los adultos en la comunidad valoran a la juventud.
8. **La juventud como un recurso**—Se le brinda a los jóvenes la oportunidad de tomar un papel útil en la comunidad.
9. **Servicio a los demás**—La gente joven participa brindando servicios a su comunidad una hora o más a la semana.
10. **Seguridad**—Los jóvenes se sienten seguros en casa, en la escuela y en el vecindario.

**Límites y expectativas**

11. **Límites familiares**—La familia tiene reglas y consecuencias bien claras, además vigila las actividades de los jóvenes.
12. **Límites escolares**—En la escuela proporciona reglas y consecuencias bien claras.
13. **Límites vecinales**—Los vecinos asumen la responsabilidad de vigilar el comportamiento de los jóvenes.
14. **El comportamiento de los adultos como ejemplo**—Los padres y otros adultos tienen un comportamiento positivo y responsable.
15. **Compañeros como influencia positiva**—Los mejores amigos del (la) joven son un buen ejemplo de comportamiento responsable.
16. **Altas expectativas**—Ambos padres y maestros motivan a los jóvenes para que tengan éxito.

**Uso constructivo del tiempo**

17. **Actividades creativas**—Los jóvenes pasan tres horas o más a la semana en lecciones de música, teatro u otras artes.
18. **Programas juveniles**—Los jóvenes pasan tres horas o más a la semana practicando algún deporte, o en organizaciones en la escuela o de la comunidad.

**19. Comunidad religiosa**—Los jóvenes pasan una hora o más a la semana en actividades organizadas por alguna institución religiosa.

**20. Tiempo en casa**—Los jóvenes conviven con sus amigos "sin nada especial que hacer" dos o pocas noches por semana.

## ELEMENTOS FUNDAMENTALES INTERNOS

**Compromiso con el aprendizaje**

**21. Motivación por sus logros**—El (La) joven es motivado(a) para que salga bien en la escuela.

**22. Compromiso con la escuela**—El (La) joven participa activamente con el aprendizaje.

**23. Tarea**—El (La) joven debe hacer su tarea escolar por lo menos durante una hora cada día de clases.

**24. Preocuparse por la escuela**—Al (A la) joven debe importarle su escuela.

**25. Leer por placer**—El (La) joven lee por placer tres horas o más por semana.

**Valores positivos**

**26. Preocuparse por los demás**—El (La) joven valora ayudar a los demás.

**27. Igualdad y justicia social**—Para el (la) joven tiene mucho valor el promover la igualdad y reducir el hambre y la pobreza.

**28. Integridad**—El (La) joven actúa con convicción y defiende sus creencias.

**29. Honestidad**—El (La) joven "dice la verdad aún cuando esto no sea fácil".

**30. Responsabilidad**—El (La) joven acepta y toma responsabilidad por su persona.

**31. Abstinencia**—El (La) joven cree que es importante no estar activo(a) sexualmente, ni usar alcohol u otras drogas.

**Capacidad social**

**32. Planeación y toma de decisiones**—El (La) joven sabe cómo planear y hacer elecciones.

**33. Capacidad interpersonal**—El (La) joven es sympático, sensible y hábil para hacer amistades.

**34. Capacidad cultural**—El (La) joven tiene conocimiento de y sabe convivir con gente de diferente marco cultural, racial o étnico.

**35. Habilidad de resistencia**—El (La) joven puede resistir la presión negativa de los compañeros así como las situaciones peligrosas.

**36. Solución pacífica de conflictos**—El (La) joven busca resolver los conflictos sin violencia.

**Identidad positiva**

**37. Poder personal**—El (La) joven siente que él o ella tiene el control de "las cosas que le suceden".

**38. Auto-estima**—El (La) joven afirma tener una alta auto-estima.

**39. Sentido de propósito**—El (La) joven afirma que "mi vida tiene un propósito".

**40. Visión positiva del futuro personal**—El (La) joven es optimista sobre su futuro mismo.

some of the assets are very important while others seem less so, and in fact you can think of assets that should be on the list in place of some of the ones that are there now. That's fine, too. There's nothing magical about these particular assets except for the important fact that they're the ones whose associations with young people's success have been borne out in research. It's not mere opinion; it's data. There may be more than 40 developmental assets, but they haven't been identified yet.

Given the evidence that these assets are important, Search Institute naturally wanted to know how prevalent they were. So it administered surveys to students in grades 6–12 in communities across the country to see how many assets they reported experiencing. It turns out that on average, young people report having about 19—and, discouragingly, the older of the young people report having fewer assets than the younger of the young people. Obviously, all assets are not created equal, and for some people some assets are more important than others. Nonetheless, unless you're a baseball player, 19 out of 40 does not yield a good percentage, so I think we can agree on a second point: **Young people need more assets.**

Where do young people get these assets? If you review the list, it won't surprise you that young people get many of them from adults—their parents, their teachers, the people in their community. Building many of the external assets, in fact, is almost entirely dependent on adults. If you're an adult and you spend a lot of time with a young person—as you most likely do if you're connected with an organization that serves youth—then you're in a good position to build assets with that young person. Note that I said build assets *with,* not *for,* that young person. Assets don't come in syringes; you can't inject them like vaccines. Young people have to be part of building the assets themselves. You can help, of course, and I hope to show you how in the forthcoming pages. But it's essential to recognize that in the end this is not something you can do alone.

There are at least three major ways you can help build assets, and you'll be pleased to know that the most important way is something you may already do. The first way to build assets with a young person is to have a good relationship with that young person.

This is obvious, I know, but it's so important that I want to make it our third point: **Young people need good relationships with adults.** The reason it's so important is that if you have a good relationship with a young person, then you're more credible when you impart information, lend

Figure 1.3

# The Power of Assets to Promote and Protect

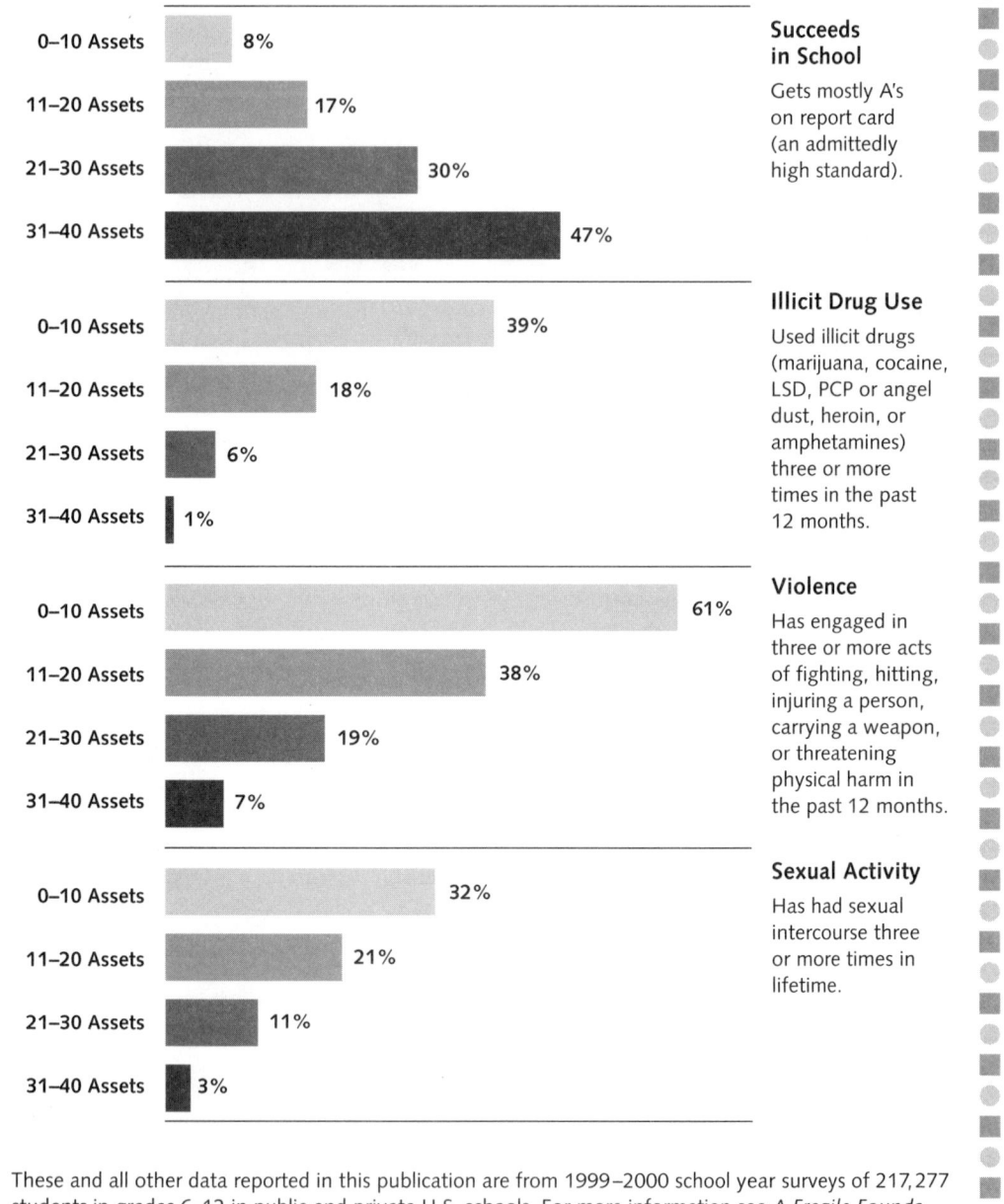

**0–10 Assets** 8%
**11–20 Assets** 17%
**21–30 Assets** 30%
**31–40 Assets** 47%

**Succeeds in School**

Gets mostly A's on report card (an admittedly high standard).

**0–10 Assets** 39%
**11–20 Assets** 18%
**21–30 Assets** 6%
**31–40 Assets** 1%

**Illicit Drug Use**

Used illicit drugs (marijuana, cocaine, LSD, PCP or angel dust, heroin, or amphetamines) three or more times in the past 12 months.

**0–10 Assets** 61%
**11–20 Assets** 38%
**21–30 Assets** 19%
**31–40 Assets** 7%

**Violence**

Has engaged in three or more acts of fighting, hitting, injuring a person, carrying a weapon, or threatening physical harm in the past 12 months.

**0–10 Assets** 32%
**11–20 Assets** 21%
**21–30 Assets** 11%
**31–40 Assets** 3%

**Sexual Activity**

Has had sexual intercourse three or more times in lifetime.

These and all other data reported in this publication are from 1999–2000 school year surveys of 217,277 students in grades 6–12 in public and private U.S. schools. For more information see *A Fragile Foundation: The State of Developmental Assets among American Youth;* and *Developmental Assets: A Synthesis of the Scientific Research on Adolescent Development,* both available from Search Institute.

support, or offer advice. I'm not going to expand on what I mean by a "good relationship" right now, but I think it'll become clear as you read the stories and examples in this book and take note of what people are doing around the country.

The second way to build assets with a young person is to provide a positive, challenging, supportive environment. Again, this will become clearer as you read the book, but think for a moment about what kind of environment *you* thrive in—at work, at home, in your community. What does it look, sound, and feel like? You probably know it when you're in it: You feel that you matter, that everyone's on your side, that, despite obstacles, you can succeed—however you define "success." So our fourth point should go without saying (but it won't): **Young people need supportive environments.**

The third way to build assets is to provide programs and activities that give young people opportunities to thrive. No doubt you're familiar with such programs and activities, although maybe you haven't thought of them from this perspective. While you can certainly build assets without programs, programs can set parameters in which groups of young people excel. Generally, if people can learn something from an activity, feel good about themselves, and even benefit others, then the activity is probably building assets. Young people also need the opportunity within these programs and activities to try new things, to fail, to be accepted when they fail, to recover, and to redouble their efforts to succeed. Point 5: **Young people need programs and activities that are conducive to building assets.**

Maybe you already "know" most of this. Maybe you're even translating that knowledge into actions. Maybe your organization is helping young people build assets left and right. But take a look at Figure 1.4 and see which column more accurately describes your organization.

If you find yourself more familiar with the left-hand column, then there's a lot of information in this book that you'll probably find useful. If you find yourself more familiar with the right-hand column, then congratulations! But I bet you can still pick up some pointers, new ideas, and new inspiration.

The upshot is this: If you work in an organization that serves young people, you're in a great position to build assets. Whether you do more administering than interacting, work directly with young people, or are less directly involved with such an organization—say, a board member

*Which assets do you think the young people you know need most?*

*Which assets do you feel most comfortable in helping young people build?*

### Figure 1.4

# Becoming an Asset-Rich Organization

| An Asset-Poor Organization | An Asset-Rich Organization |
|---|---|
| 1. Focus is on young people's problems. | 1. Focus is on young people's strengths and on using those strengths to deal with problems. |
| 2. Only certain people in the organization believe they can help young people build assets. | 2. Everyone in the organization believes they can help young people build assets. |
| 3. Young people absorb resources. | 3. Young people are resources. |
| 4. Building developmental assets is a program. | 4. Building developmental assets is a way to interact with young people. |
| 5. The organization tries to affect primarily those young people who seem to be troubled or who are causing trouble. | 5. The organization tries to affect all the young people who come into contact with it every day. |
| 6. How adults outside the organization behave around young people isn't a concern. | 6. All adults are held accountable for their actions toward young people. |
| 7. The belief is, "We already build assets." | 7. The belief is, "We need to build assets more intentionally." |
| 8. It's okay to blame others for young people's poor behavior. | 8. It's unacceptable to blame others for the past. The focus is on working with others to improve the future. |

or a bus driver, a consultant or a parent—this book is for you. And if you are a young person, you're also in a great position to build assets: for yourself, with your peers, and—don't make a big deal of this—with adults.

## Asset Builders

*"I say hi and good-bye to every passenger, even the kids with spiked hair."*

—ED deBOER, bus driver and crisis-line volunteer, Victoria, British Columbia

Asset builders are all around us. Some of them we notice right away—the youth worker who "has a way with kids"; the parent who goes out of her way to say hi to everyone on her son's soccer team; the program coordinator who's always on the lookout to expand his organization's services. Other people may be "stealth asset builders"—the secretary whom, for some reason, students trust; the teenager who quietly tutors a second-grade special ed. student; the curriculum developer who constantly strives to create activities in which young people are the driving force, not the recipient; and the bus driver, like Ed deBoer, who views her or his role as more than just providing transportation. People build assets in different ways, and thank goodness—because we're all receptive to different strategies.

*Which people around you—adults and young people—are "natural" asset builders?*

You'll meet a lot of asset builders in this book, many of them of the "stealth" variety. The people included are not necessarily the ones who are "spreading the word" about developmental assets, though some of them are. Awareness is certainly one of the parents of change—but only one. I've tried to focus on people who are doing something concrete to build assets with young people, maybe even doing something differently because of assets. They're walking their talk.

*How could you enlist them to be more intentional with their efforts?*

And that's what I'd like you to do, too.

# 2
# Walking
# Relationships

Tommy Tinajero sits across from me in an El Paso restaurant trying to explain the success of the Paso del Norte Health Foundation. He doesn't really have to convince me, because in the past day or two I've seen and heard enough to know that the people in this little area that encompasses corners of Texas, New Mexico, and Mexico are doing more to build assets than almost any other place in the United States. I think he may be trying to understand the success himself. Over a lunch of tacos and enchiladas, we've been talking about assets and programs and partnerships and budgets and, especially, individual relationships between adults and young people. And then he puts down his fork, looks directly at me, and says, "The messages are behind the relationships." I think about that for a second, and I know he's right. The messages are behind the relationships. How simple. The messages are behind the relationships.

# What Young People Want

*"It's good going to sleep at night knowing you've done something*

*for your community."*

—ALEXANDRA RODRIGUEZ, AmeriCorps member

I've talked with many young people across the country who are in some way involved with organizations that serve youth. I've talked with residents of the Christie House in Marylhurst, Oregon, who have come from some of the least asset-rich environments you can imagine. I've talked with members of the Promoting Assets Across Cultures (PAAC) Team in Seattle, whose participation in the group is a viable alternative to a life on the street with drugs and violence. I've talked with students from the El Paso region, many of them poised between two cultures and whose sense of extended family is a strong asset indeed.

And what do these young people say they want?

They want to be listened to. They want to be supported when they make mistakes as well as recognized when they succeed. They want to learn about themselves and about each other. They want to be challenged, to be taught useful information and skills. They want to be valued—for who they are, not for what people think teenagers are like. They want to give something to their communities.

And they want adults to be *real*—to walk their talk.

Many of these young people know little about the developmental assets framework, but they can easily articulate what it means to have assets and what it means not to have assets. Let me give you some examples of how they expressed that:

**Young people want to be listened to.** How simple is that? And yet being listened to is apparently not something to which many youth are accustomed. A young woman from metropolitan Minneapolis's Mosaic Youth Center, which recently published *Step by Step! A Young Person's Guide to Positive Community Change*, almost plaintively said, "This is the first group where I've ever been able to be myself, voice my opinion."

**Young people want to be supported when they make mistakes as well as recognized when they succeed.** The Christie School is Oregon's oldest and largest residential treatment center. It's a beautiful facility; when you walk the grounds, you get the feeling that it could be a small private college, not a residence for 82 young people ages 8 to 18, 80 percent of them with a history of horrific abuse and neglect. Christie is, on the average, these young people's 14th out-of-home placement.

A teenage resident of the Christie School woke up one morning and declared that she wasn't going to classes that day. "They could have blown me off," she said—threatened her with dire consequences, forced her to attend classes, or thrown up their hands and left her in her room. But the staff worked with her, reasoned with her, sought compromise; she ended up promising to attend morning classes and then to decide what she wanted to do after that. This young woman values apologizing and taking responsibility for her actions, both of which she did, and both of which she expects adults to do when it's appropriate.

**Young people want to learn about themselves and about each other.** Solomon Abay is vice president of Seattle's PAAC Team. At first he derided the team, thought it was for "losers." But then he realized that not only were people involved with the team telling him that life isn't worthwhile without schooling, they also were backing it up with practical information and connections with potential employers. Abay got motivated in a way echoed by the young people in an El Paso AmeriCorps program: When new people join a group, at first they're motivated by the others in the group, and then they don't want to let the others down. They themselves become models.

**Young people want to be challenged, to be taught useful information and skills.** Peer pressure is sometimes seen as negative, but when a young person's peer is building assets, the pressure is positive. Gail Vessels, vice president of organizational effectiveness of the Boys and Girls Clubs of Greater Kansas City, tells the story of a teenager who was approaching high school graduation but struggling with math. He'd received a preliminary college scholarship that would be withdrawn if he didn't get at least a B in his math class. So Vessels found a tutor for the boy, which paid off: The boy earned an A in his math class and went on to college. Fine for the boy, but even better for his friends: Upon seeing what happened, they all decided that they wanted their own tutors.

**Young people want to be valued.** The Community Youth Employment Program (CYEP), sponsored by the Fund for the City of New York, gives young people opportunities to explore their goals and to be valued for who they are. CYEP is implemented in several sites in Manhattan and the Bronx for seven weeks every July and August; a coordinator guides the work of 8–12 young people at each site. Working in the program for 30 hours per week, participants are trained and employed in community assessment and development activities. Read what some of the youth from the program have to say, this from the December 1999 Program Evaluation Report:

> ➤ "I am a really quiet person and I never had a job before. The people here have pushed me to speak out, to make decisions, and that's good because I'm learning how to deal with the real world."
> ➤ "I thought we had things already planned for us; then I found out we had to come up with our own ideas."
> ➤ "I learned this is not summer school. You took on a responsibility; now you have to do the work."

**Young people want to give something to their communities.** So far, this is what we might expect: Youth revel in being given responsibility. People responding to them as valued resources have an effect on their self-perceptions as valued resources. But now read the following, from the same CYEP young people:

*Have you asked young people what they want from your organization?*

> ➤ "I learned a lot about teamwork. The program made me want to give back to my community."
> ➤ "I was very lazy and not motivated. Now I'm helping people because I've learned a lot and feel I can give something back to people."
> ➤ "CYEP made me more aware of what is going on in the community and will make me a better leader and advocate for my peers."

*Have you asked them what they have to offer your organization?*

*Have you given them the opportunity to provide you with feedback on what you've been doing?*

*Do you really listen to them?*

There's a strong undercurrent among teenagers of a desire to help others. They recognize this in themselves. When the PAAC Team brings in new members, they ask them first what they can do to help the community. To these young people, meeting the needs of their community is paramount—even if, as one teenager said, the media don't show up. Matthew C. Franklin, a college student formerly associated with a Pennsylvania Healthy Communities • Healthy Youth Initiative, says, "Adults really can get past the idea that youth don't know what is going on and in turn see that we do care about the community."

This section of Chapter 2 is deliberately short. I could sum it up in two words, the response to the question posed by the title. What do young people want? *Ask them.*

# Changing the Rules

*"I have yet to meet a young person interested in being 'prevented.' "*

—RICK JACKSON, former vice president, YMCA of Greater Seattle

Ask a young person to describe a typical dynamic with an adult, and you may be surprised at how "asset-poor" it is—even if the young person doesn't recognize it as such. Nancy Gruver believes that this is especially true of relationships between adults and girls, the latter of whom are often relegated to even lower rungs of responsibility than are boys. Gruver is the founder of New Moon Publishing, a company in Duluth, Minnesota, in which girls 8–14 years old and adults together produce a bimonthly magazine called *New Moon: The Magazine for Girls and Their Dreams*. The girls' editorial board meets twice a month on Sunday afternoons with adult coworkers; they make all the important decisions regarding the magazine, including selecting articles written by girls from around the world. When the girls turn 15, they "retire" and the board chooses their replacements.

The magazine itself is a compendium of articles of interest to girls. A recent issue included the following:

- ➤ "Butt-Kickin' Babes of the Golden Age"—women warriors and the people who love them;
- ➤ "Shake Your Beauty!"—a call to submit the names of girls who are beautiful just by being themselves;
- ➤ "Deliver Me"—a short history of midwifery;
- ➤ "The Truth about Aunt Flo"—myths and superstitions about menstruation; and
- ➤ "Aped Crusaders"—a profile of the Guerrilla Girls, an undercover group of professional women artists in New York who protest discrimination in the arts.

*New Moon* also includes regular features like poetry, advice columns, art, discussions of issues, and opinions. "My mission is to bring girls' voices into the public discourse with respect," says Gruver. To illustrate that, *New Moon* has produced two lists of "rules for relationships" between adults and girls. As you read the lists in Figure 2.1, think about your own attitudes as well as those of your coworkers, and see which set of rules you're more familiar with.

Figure 2.1

# Changing the Rules

### The Usual Rules for Relationships between Adults and Girls

➤ Don't be honest with girls—they can't handle it.

➤ Girls can't understand adult feelings and experiences.

➤ Don't let girls challenge adults.

➤ Don't challenge girls.

➤ Girls need to be taken care of by adults.

➤ Girls need to be left alone by adults.

➤ Girls don't have anything important to say.

➤ Girls don't understand their own experience.

➤ Girls can't handle complexity.

➤ Girls don't know what real life (and real disappointment) is.

➤ Girls aren't interested in talking with adults.

➤ Girls don't listen.

➤ Girls are irresponsible, frivolous, and petty, absorbed in childish pursuits.

### The New Rules: Share the Power

➤ Everyone is responsible for a common goal. Therefore, everyone shares the meaningful work.

➤ Have a real interest in the work. Be committed to it and to each other.

➤ Listening comes first for the adults, and talking comes first for the girls.

➤ Not talking is okay, but not listening is not okay.

➤ Actively seek and encourage girls' opinions.

➤ Welcome disagreement but end in compromise.

➤ Discuss—don't force—ideas. Be willing to be persuaded by others in discussion.

➤ Express your deep feelings passionately, and if something isn't too important to you personally, defer to someone who does have very strong feelings.

➤ No one knows all the answers.

➤ Be open to learning from each other.

➤ Make decisions with girls, not for them. This takes more time!

➤ Be honest and build trust. Respect each other and each other's opinions.

➤ Don't be condescending.

➤ Be supportive, encouraging, positive, realistic, and patient.

➤ Be responsive to your group's needs. Be aware of nonverbal cues.

➤ Make meetings girl-friendly:

 • Have a set time to start and finish.

 • Meet at a time when girls do not have other commitments (like school).

 • Arrange the seating so that no one is in a position of power; sit in a circle, on the same level.

 • If the meeting is longer than 60 minutes, take a break for snacks and physical activity.

 • Allow social time.

 • Come organized. Write tasks down for the whole group.

Created by New Moon Publishing. Used by permission in *Walking Your Talk: Building Assets in Organizations That Serve Youth*, by Neal Starkman. Copyright © 2002 by Search Institute, 800-888-7828, www.search-institute.org.

The rules—"usual" as well as "new"—are basically about creating mutual respect and trust, and can apply to any adult-teenager relationship. It looks almost obvious on paper, but ask young people how obvious it is when they interact with adults.

Is this the totality of walking your talk in relationships—treating teenagers with respect? Is building assets as simple as going down the list of 40 and making sure that you're giving as many assets as you can to as many young people as you can? Of course not. Keep in mind that you can't force a positive relationship; the relationship has to be mutual. So let's for a moment talk about an important concept I don't want to pass over. There's a built-in tension between the desire on the part of adults to build assets for young people and, on the other hand, the need for young people to take responsibility to develop their own assets.

As I stated in Chapter 1, you can't just *give* assets to young people. What you *can* do is to provide them with an environment, with opportunities, with tools so that they can build the assets for themselves. It's not just semantics. I can provide what I think is positive family communication, but I can't make my child seek advice or counsel from me. I can teach teenagers how to resist negative peer pressure and dangerous situations, but I can't accompany them to parties and force them to use those resistance skills. And I can constantly tell the young people in my charge that they're wonderful and capable and smart, but they're the ones who will have to believe it.

I repeat: That's why we in the asset-building business say that we need to build assets *with* young people, not *for* them. We can forge the relationships, we can set up the environment, and we can implement the programs and the activities, but the change has to come from within the young person. For some of us, "changing the rules" means backing off: engaging with young people rather than providing for them, and trusting them to do good things for themselves.

Heidi Struve-Harvey, community outreach specialist for the Washoe County Department of Juvenile Services in Reno, Nevada, offers us a good example of this approach to building assets. It's a tool that she uses to guide young people in building their own assets. They are asked to choose an asset and give a detailed description of the steps they plan to take to build it. Talk about responsibility: Take a look at Figure 2.2 and see how easy it would be for *you* to complete it.

### Figure 2.2

## Individual Action Plan

Student Name: _____

Date: _____

Name of the asset I choose to work on: _____

1. Describe your reasons for choosing this asset. _____

2. List some things you will need to do to start building this asset—be very specific. _____
   _____

3. Go through your list of things and put them in order—what has to be done first, second, third, etc. _____
   _____

4. Describe when you will start working on this asset. List the day, date, and time. _____
   _____

5. Describe how often you need to work on this asset. _____
   _____

6. Describe where you need to work on this asset. _____
   _____

7. List some people whom you would like to help you build this asset. _____
   _____

8. Describe how you will ask them for help. _____
   _____

9. Pick a time to reflect on your progress toward building this asset. List the day, date, and time you will do this. _____
   _____

10. Describe how you will celebrate if you are successful in building this asset (remember that this celebration doesn't have to cost money). _____
    _____

11. If you are not successful on your first try, whom will you go to for help in trying again? _____
    _____

12. What message will you think of to motivate yourself to keep trying? You might want to write this down somewhere you can see it every day. _____
    _____
    _____

Note that the young person does all the work—deciding which asset to work on, starting to build the asset, determining where and when to build the asset, deciding where to get support, and planning how to both celebrate successes and persist in the face of setbacks. But the nature of the adult relationships is sometimes elusive. The idea behind an asset-rich relationship isn't to "prevent" problems for the young person. An adult needs to be there to support, to guide, to celebrate with, and to motivate—but not to dominate. "Walking your talk" in an asset-rich relationship means that the adult often has to cede some power, control, and responsibility to the young person.

## Mentoring

*Mentors are good listeners, people who care, people who want to help young people bring out strengths that are already there.*
—NATIONAL MENTORING PARTNERSHIP

Probably the most effective bridges between asset-rich relationships and asset-rich activities are mentoring programs. These programs can take many forms in a variety of venues, but their essence is a relationship between two people in which one person imparts information, support, or guidance to the other. The National Mentoring Partnership (www. mentoring.org) gives some examples of what mentors might do:

➤ Plan a project for school.

➤ Explore a topic of mutual interest.

➤ Visit some of the exciting places where you live.

➤ Set some career goals and start taking steps to make them happen.

➤ Learn more about the community and how to help others through volunteering.

➤ Strengthen communication skills and ability to relate well to all kinds of people.

➤ Make healthy choices about day-to-day life, from food to exercise and beyond.

There are many different kinds of mentoring programs. Some of them are very formal, in which the mentor and mentee meet on a regular basis and

*What rules guide the relationships between the adults and young people in your organization?*

*Do the rules need to change?*

*How would that happen?*

address predetermined issues. Others are more casual: The mentor is "there" for the mentee when needed and occasionally when not needed. Some mentoring programs use "ghost" mentors: Adults select young people who they perceive need guidance and support, but no formal relationship is ever established; the young people aren't even aware that they're being mentored. There's also a wide variety of other facets of mentoring programs: orientation and training, selection of participants, duration of the relationship, and so on.

But the key point here is that *every* relationship between an adult and a young person can be a type of mentoring relationship. What would happen if you and the adults you work with started thinking of yourselves as mentors? How would you change? How would the relationships change? Would you "be there" more consistently? Would you be more aware of how you were affecting the young people around you?

The facilities of Portland, Oregon's Janus Youth Programs house boys and girls from 13 to 17 years old, many of whom are referred by the Oregon State Office for Services to Children and Families. I'll return to Janus later in the book, but for now consider its Youth Advancement Team's own program, called Mentoring Partners. Here is some information from a brochure that describes the program and sets the stage for a mutually rewarding mentoring relationship:

WHAT IS MENTORING PARTNERS?

The establishment of a one-on-one relationship, lasting anywhere from one and one half to three years, between a younger person (Younger Partner) and a qualified adult (Mentor).

The role [of] a Mentor is to hold the vision of success for a child beyond poverty, and to offer activities that are [in] keeping with that vision.

The role of a Younger Partner is to demonstrate respectfulness and to role model it.

The role of the Younger Partner's family is to be open and communicate well to support the match.

The role of the coordinators is to facilitate the matches, provide support to the Mentors, Younger Partners and their families, provide a monthly group activity, and support activities in the community within the program.

WHAT'S INVOLVED?

Our goal is for the Mentors to share at least two hours per week with their Younger Partners and together attend one monthly group activity. Comprehensive training is provided around various topics such as:

➤ Understanding a child's reality of poverty

➤ Learning levels of trust development

➤ Understanding appropriate methods of retaining a Mentor relationship

Ongoing support to the match relationship, the Mentors, and the Younger Partners and their families is provided by the coordinators.

One of the more unusual mentoring programs is in Minneapolis. Inner City Tennis sounds like a tennis club, and it does feature 11 tennis courts, but it's also a place for mentoring and tutoring. Seventy-three Coach Mentor Tutors recruited from the Senior Tennis Players Club, ages 55 and up, are trained to work with young people on both tennis skills and "life" skills from 5 to 15 hours each week; the young people come from Head Start and other community groups. In some ways it's like a tutoring program, but the students are learning backhand volleys instead of binomial equations.

As the National Mentoring Partnership points out, the qualities of successful mentors are these:

➤ Have a sincere desire to be involved with a young person;

➤ Respect young people;

➤ Actively listen;

➤ Empathize;

➤ See solutions and opportunities; and

➤ Be flexible and open.

You won't be surprised when I tell you that a successful mentoring relationship—whether or not it's part of a formal program—ends up building assets for the mentor as well as the mentee, especially when the mentor is a young person. Because the relationship is *mutually* respectful, *mutually* caring, and *mutually* supportive, everyone benefits.

*What kinds of mentoring—formal or informal—exist in your organization?*

*Who needs mentoring?*

*Who would make the best mentors?*

*Do you think of yourself as a mentor?*

*What would change if you did?*

*"They know if you're here just for the paycheck."*

—YOUTH WORKER IN ANTHONY, TEXAS

# 3
# Walking
# Environments

In the opening chapter of this book, I asked you to think about the kind of environment you yourself thrive in. It's probably not too different from the kind of environment in which most people—of all ages—thrive. You feel that you matter. You feel supported—guided when appropriate, left alone when appropriate. You feel that you're accepted and valued. You feel that you're challenged to do your best. Sometimes it may seem that the environment "just happened," but nothing "just happens." You feel the way you do because people act in certain ways. And people act in certain ways in part because of the beliefs they hold about themselves and each other. I hope that by now you're convinced that you want to work in an asset-rich environment and are looking for ways in which other people have created such environments. So when you read the following examples and strategies, imagine yourself—in your organization, with your young people—adapting them so that they work for you.

# The Youth Card

*"Decisions made with adults and young people are better*

*than those made with adults alone."*

—PAUL VIDAS, director, United with Youth,

Menasha, Wisconsin

In certain games there are "trump cards," those that are more powerful than any others in the deck. For youth-serving organizations seeking to build assets, engaging young people in meaningful and significant ways is a trump card of sorts. It is perhaps the most efficient and effective way to transform the organizational environment.

### Engagement

Engaging young people is notably different from simply involving them. A young person who attends a focus group about proposed activities and speaks a few words is involved. But to be engaged implies action, an assertive, take-me-seriously stance that is not always familiar or comfortable for youth or, for that matter, for adults. As it's said in regard to a bacon-and-eggs breakfast, the chicken was involved; the pig was wholly engaged.

In preparing to write this book, I talked with well over 100 people across the country, all of them working in some way with an organization that serves young people. Virtually all of the people I interviewed accepted the asset framework as a useful way to improve the lives of their young people. A proportion of those people, I believe, are intentionally and systematically building assets in some way. They do this with a variety of strategies, some of which I've already described. But no matter how much people subscribe to the framework's philosophy, no matter how many activities they facilitate that are driven by youth, the obstacle they find the most difficult to overcome is to truly engage youth by allowing them to have real decision-making power. Two outstanding exceptions are the Covington Family YMCA in Covington, Georgia, and metropolitan Minneapolis's Mosaic Youth Center; the boards of directors of both these organizations include two teenagers as voting members. There must be other examples, but in most cases, the status quo has yet to be converted to the merits of giving young people more say in their own lives, both current and future.

## Youth Councils

In the rare cases of youth participation, the young people in question invariably cut their teeth on some sort of youth council—a body of young people that plans, carries out, evaluates, and even budgets activities for their peers. Kelly Greenwell, a youth and family coordinator in Victoria, British Columbia, says that youth councils are good because they're vehicles for youth to show the community what they can do.

Youth councils abound in the Mexico, New Mexico, and Texas communities served by Paso del Norte Health Foundation in El Paso. Paso del Norte has established partnerships with schools, congregations, law enforcement organizations, businesses, and organizations, such as the local YMCA, that serve youth. One requirement for becoming a partner with Paso del Norte—and receiving funds for projects—is the existence of a youth council. At first, some organizations balked at the requirement. They were not invited to be partners in forthcoming years and were replaced by organizations who were only too happy to fill the void.

Paso del Norte uses a "Youth Council Planning Worksheet" to ask partnering organizations how they'll meet the following objectives:

1. Youth engagement through the youth council meetings;
2. Youth leadership through the youth council;
3. Youth involvement in the partnership;
4. Asset building in the partnership;
5. Participation in the Search Institute conference;
6. Asset building in the community;
7. Fund-raising;
8. Family involvement;
9. Youth recruitment; and
10. Team building.

It also asks for responses to the following questions:

➤ Describe the organizational structure of the youth council.
➤ When will youth council meetings take place?
➤ What process will be used to convene the youth council meetings?
➤ Describe communication tools and how they will be used to promote the activities of the youth council.
➤ Describe potential community service projects the youth council will implement.

► Describe how the youth council will recognize youth and asset builders from the community.

► [Describe] potential barriers to achieving the objectives of the youth council.

How would your organization meet those objectives and answer those questions, based on either a youth council you currently have or on one you might want to have? Take a few minutes to think about it before you read how the Southern Doña Ana Partnership responded to some of them:

**Objective 1. Youth engagement through the youth council meetings**—Youth will plan agendas, contact and bring together the members, recruit new youth, conduct meeting ice-breakers, and facilitate meetings. The Youth Council will use surveys of youth to measure the youth engagement in planning and conducting Youth Council meetings.

**Objective 4. Asset building in the partnership**—Youth will conduct asset activities in partnership meetings. Youth will also "adopt-an-adult" in order to develop relationships with adults in the partnership. These asset-building practices will be documented in photos, meeting agendas, and youth and adult surveys.

**Objective 8. Family involvement**—The youth council will host a family play day with games like three-legged races, volleyball, etc. This will allow the families to get to know each other a little better and to get involved in the community. Outstanding families/adult volunteers will be recognized at a partnership banquet. This will be measured with photos and a family day event survey.

**Describe the organizational structure of the youth council**—The council will vote on a President, Vice-President, Secretary, Treasurer, and a Public Relations Coordinator. Committees will include the Entrepreneurships Task Force and the Asset Promotions committee.

**[Describe] potential barriers to achieving the objectives of the youth council**—Potential barriers to achieving these objectives include negative attitudes, transportation, identifying convenient meeting locations, and lack of time/conflicts for activities.

Youth councils can come in many forms. Tricia Segal is the coordinator of young adult services at the Fort Vancouver Regional Library, in

Vancouver, Washington. Is the library a youth-serving organization? Segal serves 36,000 teenagers. We'll look at some of the programs she's facilitated in the next chapter. But in addition to developing programs, Segal began implementing young adult advisory boards; all 11 branches of the library system now have such boards.

Here is some of the text from a flyer advertising one of the advisory boards:

## YOUNG ADULT ADVISORY BOARD (YAAB)

The Young Adult Advisory Board has been created to ensure that the recreational, multicultural, educational, and social needs of teenagers are being met by the Fort Vancouver Regional Library. You can make a difference by suggesting materials, programs, and services, and by creating an environment geared towards young adults.

**Why Join?**

Community service credit

Good food

Make a difference for teens

Meet new people and have fun

**Who?**

Young adults in 9th–12th grade or 15–19 years old

From Clark, Klickitat, or Skamania Counties

**What Do We Do?**

Vancouver Mall book sale

Input on new Three Creeks branch

Help design signs, displays, logos for YAAB and YA areas

Suggest materials for the YA collection

Plan programs

Assist with Summer Reading Program

Develop a website for the YAAB

Promote our group to the community

Assist in District-wide plans—Look at the big picture

Give input to a national library committee

**When?**

2nd and 4th Tuesday of the month from 3:30–5:00 pm and at programs or projects at various times, maybe once a month

**Sharing the Power**

Youth advisory boards like the one in place at the Fort Vancouver Regional Library can be very effective, when they are well implemented and when the young people involved are truly empowered to make decisions and to be leaders. Paul Vidas believes that most youth are *not* empowered because there are greater numbers of older people who aren't willing to give up power. Vidas is a strong advocate for young people making more decisions—bad ones as well as good ones—about what affects them. As he is quoted at the beginning of this section, the core of his belief is that "decisions made with adults and young people are better than those made with adults alone." Some of those decisions turned out well for at least one town in Wisconsin. A short time after facilitating a symposium about assets with 400 teenagers, Vidas reports that the town of Freedom opened up three paid slots on its council for young people. These youth have been assigned to the Planning Committee, the Park and Recreation Committee, and the Agriculture Committee. Each receives the same per diem that adults receive, and each votes. Vidas reports that Leroy Brockman, the chair of the Planning Committee, "was surprised and pleased by the thought-provoking questions" posed by the young man on his committee.

This idea of giving up some control to youth—whether in the form of a council or even on an individual basis—is difficult for many adults to accept, and yet it's key to building an asset-rich environment, an environment in which asset builders walk their talk. By wielding some decision-making power, young people learn useful skills and become invested in the organization. Moreover, an organization with young people in the forefront is much more likely to be appealing to other young people. And another benefit, some financial icing on the cake: There is a growing understanding among foundations that programs that empower young people have more potential for success than those that don't.

What does this empowerment look like in a typical situation? How is it translated into behaviors? Earlier I mentioned Nancy Gruver, founder of *New Moon*, a magazine put together by girls and adults. I want to show you an activity that Gruver facilitates when she makes presentations and trainings to people who work with youth. She asks several participants to role-play three situations:

**Scene A:** Adults and young people getting together to decide how to spend grant money recently given to their school.

**Adults:** You are sitting in a "power" position—either at the head of rows or behind a desk. You have made all the decisions about the money together before the meeting has started. When the young people arrive, you tell them where to sit. You begin to fill them in on what your plans are for the money. As the young people respond, you ignore them, you interrupt them, and you talk to each other rather than to them. The work gets done, but the young people are notice-ably discouraged and unhappy. The assignment you give the young people for the next meeting is menial and dumb.

**Young People:** You arrive with lots of ideas about how to use the money. As you listen to the adults, you realize that you have no power in any of the decisions. As you try to voice your opinions, the adults don't listen. Eventually, you stop voicing your ideas altogether. You are dis-couraged and unhappy with the job assignment you get for the next meeting; you wish you had been given a more important job.

**Scene B:** Adults and young people getting together to decide how to spend grant money recently given to their school.

**Young People:** You show up late for the meeting, obviously not caring. You complain and whine throughout the meeting. You don't show any interest in the money. Your ideas are not practical, and you do this on purpose. You bad-mouth all ideas and each other.

**Adults:** You are obviously frustrated, yet you are not assertive with the young people—you don't confront them about their poor behavior or how it makes you feel. When you present ideas for the money, the young people are not receptive.

**Scene C:** Adults and young people getting together to decide how to spend grant money recently given to their school.

**Young People and Adults:** You sit in a circle, on the same level (e.g., every-one is in chairs or on the floor). You arrive knowing that you have a common goal. You listen to each other, without interrupting each other. Even though there is great disagreement on how to spend the money—for example, the young people want to divide the money up and buy many "little" things, like books and computers, and the adults want to use all the money to remodel and update the library— you talk it out and compromise in the end. You are open to finding solutions together. Assignments for work for the next meeting are meaningful for the young people. In the end, the meeting ends with a commitment to keep working together.

After they've acted out the scenes, participants discuss what worked and what didn't work in each situation:

### Scene A. The adults have power.
The adults are positioned in front of the young people or behind the desk.
Work gets done, but not everyone is happy.
The adults often interrupt the young people.
The adults talk to each other but not to the young people.
The adults have decisions made before the meeting.
The adults ignore the young people's ideas.
The young people are quiet and afraid to speak out.
The young people try to voice ideas, but the adults don't listen.
The young people don't share in meaningful work.

### Scene B. The young people have power.
Work doesn't get done.
The young people show up late for the meeting; they don't care.
The young people complain and whine throughout the meeting.
The young people don't show interest in planning.
The young people suggest ideas that aren't practical, and they know it.
The young people bad-mouth ideas and each other.
The adults are frustrated and not assertive with the young people.
The adults don't confront the young people about their poor behavior.

### Scene C. The young people and the adults share power.
The young people and the adults sit in a circle, on the same level.
Work gets done, and everyone is happy.
The young people and the adults listen to each other and don't interrupt.
The young people and the adults are open to finding solutions together.

The young people and the adults welcome disagreement but end
in compromise.

The young people are given meaningful work.

After the discussion, Gruver summarizes the main points: Sharing responsibility and work for a common goal and being open to listening and learning from each other are foundations for effective relationships. And these relationships, of course, are foundations for an asset-rich environment.

I present this activity because I think it's important to convey the asset-building message as realistically as possible, and role playing done well can be very realistic. People get insights that they'd never get from reading a list of the 40 developmental assets or listening to someone lecture about the need to build assets. If staff—new or seasoned—can "see the situations" before they occur, then they'll be better prepared for how to act and how not to act.

There are a myriad of ways to engage youth. As well-meaning adults with education and experience, we're sometimes convinced that were we only to explain to young people what was good for them, they'd acknowledge our wisdom and understand. But it doesn't work like that. It has never worked like that. Young people need the opportunity to fail as well as succeed, to make the wrong moves as well as the right ones, to stand up in front of an audience and be scared silly as well as triumph over their anxiety, to attend a conference and be overwhelmed as well as make friends, and to experience running a meeting and have it get totally out of hand as well as resolve seemingly insurmountable conflicts. Playing the youth card is walking your talk because it's giving youth the same opportunities and challenges you want to have.

*How do you involve youth in your organization?*

*How do you meaningfully involve youth in your organization?*

*How do your acceptance of the asset framework and your desire to help youth build assets square with your attitudes about individual young people?*

*Are you giving youth opportunities to succeed and fail?*

*Are you giving them opportunities to rise to their potential?*

## Strategies Subtle and Sublime

*"The way I implement the assets is the way I respond to kids."*

—IVORY SMITH, education specialist, Boys and Girls Clubs of King County,
Seattle, Washington

Although youth engagement can be a dramatic way of changing the environment of an organization, strategies for creating asset-rich environments can also be extremely subtle. Probably the subtlest strategies are those that focus on building the types of adult-youth relationships described in Chapter 2. For example, Ivory Smith of the Boys and Girls Clubs of King County, Washington, relates to children: She's a good listener. Many of the youth where she works are defensive, so she focuses on the areas they feel strong in, thus building their confidence. Then she gives them opportunities to use those strengths. Simple, right? Simple, maybe, but not easy.

Then how about simple *and* easy? Paul Vidas has his own set of rules when establishing friendly, supportive environments for young people. For one thing, when his group facilitates Friday night dances, he has young people and adults alike wear name tags. Why? "Anonymity," says the ever-quotable Vidas, "is an invitation to trouble."

Susan Ragsdale, a trainer for the YMCA of Middle Tennessee in Nashville, offers another example that emphasizes the importance of subtlety and flexibility in building an asset-rich environment. Teenagers and adults from the YMCA's Earth Service Corps were cleaning up a lakeside location, when a young woman who uses a wheelchair showed up unexpectedly. After some thought and discussion, four adults carried her over to a place where the water had receded and people were picking up glass. The young woman was able to point out where there was trash to be picked up and thus became a valuable member of the team. She'd never come out to a project before, and the potential was there for a very frustrating experience, but this turned out to be a memorable one instead. "She was so proud of what she did," says Ragsdale. That wouldn't have happened if adults had been thinking about the activity more than the person.

Ragsdale was also present during a community "mapping" of east Nashville that included surveying 600 businesses. The idea was to determine which businesses were supportive of young people. Stories abounded; one favorite was a barbershop in which the barber placed a candy dish as an invitation for young people to come in and talk—one of those little things that make a big difference. Other little things that make big differences: An AmeriCorps member in El Paso makes sure that after every meeting or event, he shakes hands with all the young people and thanks them for coming. Another AmeriCorps member said that one of the simplest yet most powerful things you can do to build assets is to write down what young people are saying. A third said that she makes sure to attend students' extracurricular activities and to smile at them in hallways. Simple strategies, asset-rich environments.

Part of providing an asset-rich environment is to intentionally give young people opportunities to build assets. Sissi Horton, site director of the John Muir Kids' Corner, part of Seattle's Camp Fire Boys and Girls, uses assets on her planning sheets, so that staff write how they're going to promote particular assets in activities such as crafts, kickball, and cooking; they then report back on how it went. One offshoot of this strategy for Horton's group is that she and the staff are more conscious of relationships; they no longer segregate their young people by age, and they encourage more socialization, for example, during snack time.

It doesn't take much. Tom Greenwood, a staff member at Taylor House, one of Janus Youth Programs' residential facilities in Portland, Oregon, heard some of the boys complaining about working in fast-food places, so he did something revolutionary: He asked them what they would like to do instead. Perhaps surprisingly, they said that they'd like to do silk-screening. Greenwood did some research, secured a grant, and helped the boys set up a money-making silk-screening business. And Carol White, school-age child care director of the Tillamook County Family YMCA in Tillamook, Oregon, tells the story of a girl in the fifth grade learning how to bead. She brought in her work, stoked the interest of some other children, and was soon teaching *them* how to bead. In a short period of time, she changed from a potential resource to an actual one. White was walking her talk, and so was the girl.

And sometimes you use many strategies, depending on what works with whom. David de la Fuente, director of Seattle's High Point YMCA, estimates that the young people who come to his Y—about 40 5- to 19-year-olds—experience on average 10 assets. In this Y, de la Fuente facilitates a lot of service-learning projects, for example, collecting school supplies and distributing them to students who need them; in fact, all the programs at the High Point YMCA have a give-back component. And de la Fuente believes in creating internal motivation through external reinforcement: Certain behaviors—being drug-free, getting good grades, doing a service-learning project—get members of the basketball team uniforms. One 14-year-old East African boy is a shining example of the success of this strategy. He was classically "at risk"—using drugs, fighting, getting poor grades—but de la Fuente got him on a basketball team and in a jobs program. The boy is now 21, graduated from high school, attending community college, and working as a nurse's assistant. Another of de la Fuente's stories concerns a girl from Somalia, who 10 years ago didn't even know English. But she struck up a relationship with a board member, learned English, and, as they say, blossomed; she recently graduated from the University of Washington Medical School.

### Boundaries

You want an asset-rich environment? Set up a situation in which young people can make decisions and plan activities that are meaningful to them. That, for example, is the nature of a working youth council. But there have to be boundaries—rules and norms. Marcus Stubblefield knows that. He's the coordinator of the PAAC (Promoting Assets Across Cultures) Asset Team at the SafeFutures Youth Center in the High Point community of Seattle. We earlier met the vice president, Solomon Abay, who joined the team almost reluctantly. Stubblefield is the one chosen *by* the team.

The asset team, about 25–30 teenagers, meets every Wednesday afternoon from 4:30 to 5:30 (they're planning a Friday session as well). They have a president, vice president, treasurer, and three representatives. They get together to brainstorm and plan service-learning projects and other activities, for example, potlucks with parents and new members, a police forum (because they were getting harassed), and a college forum.

Look at the guidelines and consequences that are in the contract that each person—along with Stubblefield—has to sign before becoming a member of the team:

GUIDELINES
➤ Members must respect each other.
➤ Members must use appropriate language.
➤ Members must have regular attendance for team functions and at school unless excused—may be asked to miss special trips.
➤ Members will have 2.0 GPA or above.
➤ Members must respect a difference of opinion.
➤ Members will not make fun of one's culture, name, religion, and language.
➤ Members will work as a TEAM to achieve success.
➤ Members must participate in all discussions and activities.
➤ Members will keep their hands and feet to themselves.
➤ Members will not point fingers; they will give support.

- ➤ Members will not call each other names.
- ➤ Members must respect the speaker:
- ➤ No side conversations
- ➤ No goofing off
- ➤ Members will be attentive at meetings to get things accomplished.

CONSEQUENCES

1st — Warning.

2nd — May be asked to remove yourself; upon reentry, must apologize to the group.

3rd — Clean-up or community service.

Severity of action will determine consequences.

If you're familiar with developmental assets—and, for that matter, risk factors and protective factors for high-risk behaviors—you're well aware that it's a good thing to have boundaries. One whole category of the assets relates to Boundaries and Expectations; the assets contained therein are Family Boundaries, School Boundaries, Neighborhood Boundaries, Adult Role Models, Positive Peer Influence, and High Expectations. So it should come as no surprise that young people who are aware of and accept boundaries and expectations that are fairly implemented soon internalize them. And these boundaries and expectations become the parameters of an asset-rich environment. The boundaries and expectations can be as explicit as the contract you just reviewed or as terse as the sign on one of the walls of the Loring Nicollet Bethlehem Community Center in Minneapolis: "Respect yourself. Respect others. Respect materials. Respect space."

*What strategies does your organization use to provide an asset-rich environment?*

*What boundaries exist for staff and for young people?*

*Are they aware of these boundaries?*

## Vision

*"We all need to be talking the same language."*

—DEANNA ARMSTRONG, national director of programs, services, and expansion, Camp Fire USA

It's important to have strategies, but no matter how effective they are, it's pretty tough to create a positive environment in a vacuum. Without a shared sense of what you hope for, what you're committed to, and how you plan to get it, you'll often find yourself going in circles, debating the same issues over and over again.

That shared sense is reflected in your organization's vision, mission, philosophy, and goals and objectives, and it's critical that all of the people—of all ages—in your organization know and accept them. What's even better is when the people affected by what you do are engaged in the process of shaping and articulating them.

Everything starts with a vision—a glimpse into a potential future that's shared and promulgated. In fact, the vision becomes more powerful and more useful as an increasing number of people share it. A vision provides direction and guidance. In the case of building assets, a vision lends clarity to the rationale for what people are doing, day in and day out.

Here's a vision from Janus Youth Programs Residential Facilities in Portland, Oregon: "a safe, nurturing environment wherein young men and women are empowered with tools to create positive change and incorporate effective functioning skills into their lives."

According to the literature from Janus, its programs are designed "to help all residents achieve their optimal functioning and the highest degree of independence given their age and developmental stage. Staff is trained to assist the residents as they learn to break the cycles of abuse and victimization that entrap them in behavioral dysfunction. In addition, staff work toward instilling values necessary to help each youth stay away from trouble with the law, accept responsibility for their own behaviors, and increase their independent functioning within society."

In these facilities assets are built.

Notice the language of the vision: Young men and women are *empowered*. Residents achieve a high degree of *independence*. Youth *accept responsibility for their own behaviors*. These programs don't "fix" young people; they give them the tools to maximize their strengths and their potential. As we've noted, giving young people control over what they can become is a key feature in building assets. The vision provides direction for both staff and residents.

Here's a more extensive vision that's explicitly focused on building assets. This is the vision of It's About Time for Kids, a Seattle-based initiative:

> *Our vision is of a community where young people are valued and cared for by all adults so that their lives are asset rich.*

In this world we envision, we see . . .

### Adults . . .

➤ More adults (not just professional) spend more quality time with more youth.

➤ Every adult has at least one kid he or she is wild and crazy about.

➤ Caring adults are everywhere you look.

➤ Adults are involved with kids in lots of different activities.

➤ Adults are empowered as a result of caring about children and youth.

### Young People . . .

➤ Every kid has at least one adult who is crazy about him or her.

➤ Youth are excited, hopeful, and optimistic.

➤ Youth have hopes and dreams and a plan to achieve them.

➤ Youth have opportunities to develop citizenship, rather than just prepare for it in the future.

➤ Young people are a vital, essential resource.

➤ Teens are teaching younger kids.

➤ Youth have dignity and are respected by themselves and others.

➤ Youth with family responsibilities (work, child care) are recognized.

### Organizations and Services . . .

➤ Youth agencies devote full time to asset building.

➤ Agencies, religious organizations, and schools naturally coordinate activities.

➤ Public transportation gets youth where they want to go.

➤ Young people have access to a variety of interesting, structured activities during the day and evening.

➤ There is a place in each neighborhood where asset-building activities occur (and youth employment, too).

### The Community . . .

➤ Seattle is known as the urban setting for raising kids.

➤ Elders guide adults, adults guide youth, and youth guide children.

> All streets, schools, and neighborhoods are safe.
> Policy makers budget for kids first, and then decide what is needed.
> Kids giggle, laugh, and are welcomed everywhere.
> Youth talents and achievements are displayed publicly.
> Generations are helping each other.

A vision like this spells out the desired future: Here's what it looks like ("Adults are involved with kids in lots of different activities"), here's what it sounds like ("Kids giggle, laugh, and are welcomed everywhere"), and here's what it feels like ("Youth are excited, hopeful, and optimistic"). It includes adults, youth, organizations, and the larger community, and spells out the relationships, connections, and expectations of and between all of them. This vision was created for a community-wide asset-building network, but think how useful something like this can be in an organization that serves youth: It points the way for everyone associated with that organization.

Sometimes the vision is slow in coming. Tommy Tinajero is the former program officer of Paso del Norte Health Foundation in El Paso, Texas. He's in the business of making partnerships, an important component that I'll discuss in greater detail later. Tinajero's and the foundation's original vision was to partner with schools, law enforcement agencies, faith-based organizations, clubs, businesses, and the like in a large-scale effort to make up for what they perceived as deficits and high-risk behaviors in young people, such as drug abuse. The foundation would allot grants to organizations that could reduce these deficits. At first, youth weren't included in the foundation's deliberations. Within a year or two, however, the vision changed. After becoming familiar with the developmental assets framework, Tinajero realized that he wanted to operate from a base of strengths, not deficits. He began requiring organizations to identify the assets they would build in order to receive the grants. He and his staff also started to bring in more young people, but only for "cleanup" projects, like picking up trash at city parks. Soon that changed, too. Now, Paso del Norte doesn't do anything without youth participation, and meaningful participation at that.

Sometimes the vision is thwarted. Peter Tompkins-Rosenblatt is the program director of Janus Youth Programs in Portland, Oregon. He believes in developmental assets, he believes in strength-based programming, and he believes that true "therapy" comes through everyday living (as we'll see shortly, a belief shared by the executive director of the Christie School in Marylhurst, Oregon). He also believes in the potential of the young people under his care. But Janus operates under state contracts, and the state of Oregon is not as much an adherent of strength-based programming as is Tompkins-Rosenblatt. If these kids have so many strengths, the argument goes, then why should they be kept in group homes? Tompkins-Rosenblatt knows of a 14-year-old boy with low self-esteem and serious conflicts with his family. The boy's strength is football, which also bonds him with his father. Tompkins-Rosenblatt would love to get the boy onto a football team, but he can't. The state mandates 13 hours a week of services: one hour of individual counseling; one hour of individual skill building; 10 hours of some combination of individual skill building, group skill building, individual counseling, and group counseling; and, potentially, one hour of family therapy. Beyond those hours, in-house staff need to provide daily recreation, off-campus recreation, and educational supportive services. That leaves no time for being on a football team, regardless of how therapeutic it might be. Tompkins-Rosenblatt persists, frustrated but unbowed.

A different obstacle stymied David de la Fuente, director of Seattle's High Point YMCA, for a while: low participation from parents. Many of the parents in the High Point community don't speak English. Many of them don't acknowledge institutions, such as the Y or the school, as being positive. Many of them are shy and have low self-esteem themselves. For whatever reasons, de la Fuente couldn't get enough parents to come to events like awards ceremonies. So he just expanded the invitation list. He invited representatives from nearby churches, businesses, and the YMCA Council until the crowd was of a respectable size. He realizes that there's no substitute for parents, but at least his young people were able to bask in a public showing of support when they received their awards. De la Fuente bent the rules, changed the event, in order to work toward his organization's vision for their young people.

It's not easy to make these visions a reality—it's certainly not easy for Tompkins-Rosenblatt or for de la Fuente. But it's exceedingly difficult to build assets in any organization without an initial, shared vision of what you want the end result to be.

A vision isn't a snapshot; it's a three-dimensional—no, make that a four-dimensional—movie over space and time that you can use all your

*What is the vision of your organization?*

*How consistent is it with the building of developmental assets?*

*How explicit is it— can you actually visualize what you'd like to happen?*

*How many people share this vision?*

**43**

**Figure 3.1**

# Generating a Vision

Get comfortable, close your eyes, and try to remove any distractions. Think about the young people in your organization—not necessarily as they are, but as you'd like them to be. These young people are as healthy, happy, and successful as they can be. Spend some time picturing them, watching them doing whatever they're doing, listening to them talk and interact with each other and with adults. Imagine yourself circulating among these young people, taking in everything about them—what they're doing, what they're saying, what they must be feeling. Pay attention to the entire scene, including the physical surroundings; try not to omit any details. Conjure up what you need, and observe everything. Take as much time as you need to absorb all this; then open your eyes and think about the following questions:

1. What did you see? Which young people were there? What were their names? Which adults were there? What were their names? _____

_____

_____

2. What was the location? Was it inside or outside? Was it someplace currently used by your organization? Was it someplace that your organization might conceivably acquire or create?

_____

_____

_____

3. What was everyone doing? Were people doing it by themselves? in small groups? in large groups? _____

_____

_____

4. Were there any conversations? Was there any laughter? Were people accomplishing anything? Were they struggling? Were they helping each other?_____

_____

_____

5. What do you suppose the people were feeling? _____

_____

_____

6. What did *you* feel as you were observing them?_____

_____

_____

Use the answers to these questions to forge a path toward your vision. What needs to change? *Who* needs to change? How can it happen?

senses to experience. Consider using something like the process described in Figure 3.1 to create your own vision for your organization.

## Mission

*Take time to figure out what really matters to you, because*

*whatever you decide to do is going to take some energy.*

*You're definitely going to need passion.*

—FROM STEP BY STEP! A YOUNG PERSON'S GUIDE

TO POSITIVE COMMUNITY CHANGE,

Mosaic Youth Center Board of Directors

with Jennifer Griffin-Wiesner

An organization that serves youth is not about activities; it's about youth. Neil Nicoll, the president and CEO of the YMCA of Greater Seattle, understands this distinction. He used to work primarily with numbers and activities and timelines and budgets. He still does that to some extent, but now his focus is different. Now he works primarily with helping his staff figure out what they want to accomplish in people's lives. The shift is from the activity to the person. The mission isn't so much about providing a certain number of activities or even serving a certain number of people; the mission is about the positive changes you can make in young people's lives. When children sign up now for swimming lessons at the Y, their instructors are as concerned about their ability to respect other swimmers as they are about their ability to swim across the pool. The shift from the activity to the person pays off in many ways: After taking a six-week summer school program as one of 50 students in danger of flunking sixth grade, a student said, "For the first time in my life, people have said that I'm doing things well and have encouraged me. My parents got a call each week about how well I was doing." Testimonials like that can't be measured.

William Powers, executive director of the Christie School in Marylhurst, Oregon, also understands the distinction between activities and youth. Powers says he tries to operate from a strength-based perspective, and here are some ways in which he makes concrete his mission of helping young people operate from strength:

➤ Eight to ten people participate in residents' monthly reviews of their treatment plans. The young residents themselves attend these reviews; older residents actually run them. The residents set their own objectives.

➤ Powers coordinates the Christie School of Ambassadors. Residents apply, get leadership training, give tours of the facility to visitors, and perform community service, such as working at the nearby Seniors Center, planting trees, volunteering at the Oregon Humane Society, or helping out at the local soup kitchen.

➤ Every young person has an adult as a primary advocate.

When I met with the residents of the Christie School, I was impressed with how *strong* they seemed. Remember, these are young people who have been neglected, abused, put down, and shuttled from place to place. No doubt they have many issues and problems to work through. But when they talked with me, they had strong opinions, emphasized the present and the future, spoke with pride about their accomplishments, and offered a variety of suggestions to improve their own lives and the lives of their fellow residents. It wasn't merely that they were repeating a mantra or toeing a company line; these young people were embodiments of a strength-based mission.

The Christie plan for its residents follows a four-step process, entirely consistent with the asset framework:

➤ Step 1—establishing physical safety and emotional security;

➤ Step 2—helping children to express pain;

➤ Step 3—building self-esteem; and

➤ Step 4—giving back to the community.

*What is the mission of your organization?*

*Does it motivate people to act in ways that are consistent with the asset framework?*

This could be the four-step process for any young person in any organization that serves youth: the provision of a safe place, the environment for self-expression, the building of self-esteem, and the opportunity to contribute to the community. Powers was able to fulfill his mission because he communicated it to his staff, who are committed to making it happen.

At the beginning of this book I quoted from the mission statements of Big Brothers Big Sisters of America, Boys and Girls Clubs of America, Camp Fire USA, Girl Scouts, 4-H, YMCA, and YWCA. All of the missions are inspiring. But "mission" implies movement. To be effective, the mission of your organization should not be static. It should *get people moving*.

## Philosophy

*Youth must be the central actors in their own lives.*

—FROM "YOUTH BUILDING STRONG COMMUNITIES: Community Youth Employment Program," Fund for the City of New York Youth Development Institute

"Youth must be the central actors in their own lives." It's a guiding philosophy behind the Community Youth Employment Program and should be for any organization that seeks to enrich the assets in young people's lives. It's important that these philosophies be communicated to everyone involved with the organization—just as the vision is communicated, just as the mission is communicated. The philosophy of an organization can be formed in part from the external asset categories, those that an outside source can help provide:

> ➤ **Support**—The organization provides a caring, encouraging, supportive environment.
> ➤ **Empowerment**—The organization values the young people it serves.
> ➤ **Boundaries and Expectations**—The organization gives young people responsibility and expects them to do well.
> ➤ **Constructive Use of Time**—The organization provides opportunities for young people to participate in creative, athletic, or other positive activities.

This philosophy guides the organization in its policies and the staff in their behaviors. Let's take a look at a few ways that an organization's philosophy is expressed, first from the YMCA of Greater Seattle:

The YMCA of Greater Seattle is committed to *positive youth development*. This is up-front in our mission and overall communications message: *We build strong kids, strong families, strong communities.*

The *context* of our commitment to youth is *our values*. Staff and volunteers are determined to walk our talk by demonstrating six values in our daily lives and work: *respect, responsibility, honesty, caring, faith, fun.*

In all that we do, Seattle YMCA volunteers and staff are committed to:

➤ Teach youth positive skills, values, and an ethic of service
➤ Support and strengthen families
➤ Develop health in spirit, mind, and body
➤ Offer quality experiences that are affordable and efficiently managed
➤ Encourage participation by all members of our community
➤ Create an environment where everyone aspires to be their best

The Seattle YMCA embraces an "asset-building" approach to positive youth development. This calls for everyone in the community to work together to provide young people with the developmental building blocks they need to be successful in life.

Where does the philosophy of the YMCA end and the philosophy of the asset framework begin? It's seamless. Could your organization adopt a philosophy such as this one? Hasn't it already?

I've been mentioning Janus Youth Programs, the residential treatment facilities in the Portland, Oregon, area. Janus's two main facilities are Clackamas House, which serves up to 10 teenage girls, and Taylor House, which serves up to seven teenage boys. These young people come to the houses with a variety of issues—posttraumatic stress disorder, major depression, conduct disorder, adjustment disorder, and oppositional defiant behaviors—and histories of sexual, physical, and emotional abuse. The staff—a program director, program supervisor, direct care staff, and social service staff, with an auxiliary staff of psychiatrist, school personnel, administrative staff, and volunteers—provide supervision 24 hours a day, seven days a week. Here's one way in which these two houses communicate their philosophy to their young clients:

**Activity-Based:** This means that we believe that effective treatment occurs through daily activities and life events as opposed to just sitting around and talking.

**Solution-Focused:** This means that instead of focusing on what we think are your problems, we want to assist you in finding your solutions.

**Relationship-Oriented:** This means that we rely more on trust and communication than we do on points and levels.

Another component of Janus Youth Programs is the Columbia Villa/ Tamarack Youth Advancement Team, facilitated by Tillie MakePeace. The team is part of a consortium of agencies serving Oregon's largest low-income housing community. The philosophy of the team is expressed in this list of values:

> Every person is as equally wonderful as I am wonderful.
> Each of us is our own best resource.
> A family's best resource is within the family.
> Mutually respectful interaction is imperative.
> Never give up on anybody, including ourselves.
> Fun is as important as problem solving.
> Role modeling is the most powerful teacher.
> Self-care is the foundation of all resiliency.

And the Victoria Boys and Girls Clubs Services of Greater Victoria, British Columbia, communicates its philosophy by separating it into areas that very much resemble some of the developmental assets:

**We care about children and youth**

Boys and Girls Clubs' services are available to all young people. Our organization believes children and youth need special support to overcome disadvantages. Young people naturally seek excitement, friendship, and support. Happily, the chance to offer encouragement, direction, and counseling comes as a result of gaining their trust.

**Sense of self-worth**

We hold that an individual's sense of self-worth is fundamental, and Boys and Girls Clubs support this basic value.

**Children and youth need to be heard**

We believe every young person has the right to be listened to . . . to be heard and responded to, as someone who really matters and as someone whose ideas could make a difference.

**Acceptance and sense of belonging**

We acknowledge the need of all young people to be accepted and liked, and to become competent, both among their peers and in the eyes of adults. We are sensitive to the isolation of the individual who is different in any way, and we endeavour to create in our services an atmosphere that fosters a sense of belonging and acceptance.

### Appreciation of cultural differences

Boys and Girls Clubs encourage and foster cross-cultural understanding and appreciation. Our programs are accessible to all youth and reflect the ever-changing needs of youth and families in our communities.

### Empowerment and potential

We believe that all children and youth have the right to maximize their potential by experiencing challenges and responsibilities typical of healthy family and community life. We know young people attain their highest levels of personal growth and development when they are empowered to achieve a balance between "giving to" and "receiving from" their community. Boys and Girls Clubs encourage community service, self-help, and self-sufficiency by presenting challenges and fostering responsibility and authority in children and youth.

### Learning

We recognize that learning plays a significant role in the development of children and youth. We support, foster, and encourage life-long learning.

### Sense of adventure

We understand the natural desire young people have to be challenged by risk and adventure, to seek recognition and blaze new trails, to climb rugged mountain slopes just to stand a few moments on the highest peak, to perform in a play, or to rocket to the moon.

### Importance of the family

We recognize that family—a young person's network—is the most influential context in which children and youth learn. Our encouragement and support of the caring role in this process are imperative.

### Importance of role models

Role models play an important role in young people's lives. Boys and Girls Clubs search out and support those who model honesty, enthusiasm, fair play, respect, tolerance, and forgiveness.

### Commitment to volunteers

Boys and Girls Clubs value volunteers. Our management and service structures reflect this commitment. The involvement and support of volunteers are essential to the maintenance of socially and economically responsible programs.

### Cooperation

Boys and Girls Clubs will cooperate with families, other service organ-

izations, and governments to most effectively address the needs of children and youth.

### Neighbourhood and community

We believe that neighbourhood- and community-based approaches
that reach out to children, youth, and families hold the greatest potential for fulfilling our mission.

### Advocacy

Boys and Girls Clubs advocate positions and actions which further the
common good of children, families, and community.

You may have noticed that the full name of this organization is Boys
and Girls Clubs *Services* of Greater Victoria. According to Executive
Director Ralph Hembruff, the change from simply Boys and Girls Clubs
was entirely deliberate. It represents a shift that occurred after a crisis
in the community and is reflected in the positive framing of their philosophical statements. In 1998, a child was murdered by other children. In
seeking to determine why it happened and to prevent similar acts from
occurring, the shocked community convened a conference focusing on
developmental assets and broadcast it live on a local cable station and
radio station. One result of this new focus on strengths rather than
deficits was the combining of the Boys and Girls Clubs with Coastal
Community Services, a corrections institution; hence, Boys and Girls
Clubs Services. Hembruff's organization does a lot of work with the
criminal justice system, in addition to serving more than 2,500 young
people in the greater Victoria area.

Perhaps nowhere is the philosophy of an organization that serves
youth under the banner of developmental assets more astutely presented
than just east of Victoria, at the Boys and Girls Clubs of British Columbia, in Vancouver. Regional Director Keith Pattinson says that 10 years
ago, he took a long, hard look at his organization. What, he asked himself, do we really do? He discovered, just as we've been discussing, that
the focus was too much on programs and not enough on people. In the
following decade, Pattinson collaborated with schools across the province
as well as the provincial justice department to spread the strength- and
caring-based philosophy of the developmental assets framework. The following article appeared in the summer 2001 issue of the *Asset Building
Networker*, published by Boys and Girls Clubs of British Columbia. It
illustrates nicely Pattinson's philosophy of focusing on people.

The following is something to make us stop and think. Take this quiz:

1. Name the five wealthiest people in the world.
2. Name the last five Heisman trophy winners.
3. Name the last five winners of the Miss America contest.
4. Name ten people who have won the Nobel or Pulitzer prize.
5. Name the last half dozen Academy Award winners for best actor and actress.
6. Name the last decade's World Series winners.

How did you do? The point is, none of us remember the headliners of yesterday. These are no second-rate achievers. They are the best in their fields. But the applause dies. Awards tarnish. Achievements are forgotten. Accolades and certificates are buried with their owners.

Here's another quiz. See how you do on this one:

1. List a few teachers who aided your journey through school.
2. Name three friends who have helped you through a difficult time.
3. Name five people who have taught you something worthwhile.
4. Think of a few people who have made you feel appreciated and special.
5. Think of five people you enjoy spending time with.
6. Name half a dozen heroes whose stories have inspired you.

Easier? The lesson? The people who made a difference in your life are not the ones with the most credentials, the most money, or the most awards. They are the ones [who] care.

**A Youth Development Approach**

I've previously referred to New York's Community Youth Employment Program. It uses a "youth development" approach. See if this philosophy sounds familiar to you:

Developing youth in positive ways entails viewing them in terms of their developmental progress, considering their strengths, and providing opportunities and experiences that will enhance their further growth and development. In contrast to a deficit model that focuses on weaknesses and tries to "fix" what is wrong or eliminate deficiencies, the youth development approach uses strategies that provide young people with the following:

➤ A healthy, safe environment

➤ A wide variety of challenging activities, opportunities, and experiences that help to develop life skills

➤ Enduring relationships with caring adults who have high expectations of youth

➤ Involvement in planning and designing their own development

➤ Interactions in a community that is broader than family

➤ Opportunities for reflection and self-assessment

In other words, a youth development framework concentrates on providing and/or strengthening those components in the lives of youth that are associated with their healthy growth and development. The philosophical underpinnings of the framework do not ignore weaknesses and risk behaviors but instead recognize that well-developed positive attributes act as a buffer to strengthen areas of weakness and diminish the chance that youth will engage in unhealthy or risky behaviors.

The preceding description was taken from the Community Youth Employment Program Evaluation Report, but with a few slight edits it could easily have come from a Search Institute publication. The report goes on to say that "while few youth development advocates and educators question the importance of supporting youth in positive ways, there is much less agreement about the particular ways this can be done and at what venues." What I'm suggesting in this book is that the developmental assets framework provides an excellent way of supporting youth—in practically any venue. When young people find themselves in an environment that brings out their strengths and potential, then they're in an asset-rich environment.

Why am I presenting these different philosophical statements? Look back at them; they all reflect a dedication to building on strengths, to giving young people control over their lives, to encouraging service to others, and to providing strong relationships between young people and

*What is the philosophy of your organization?*

*What values does it espouse?*

*Does it focus on strengths?*

*Does it focus on young people?*

*Does it focus on relationships?*

adults. The precursor to "walking your talk" is "knowing your talk"—getting everyone involved to hold similar philosophical positions. Only then can you begin to carry out the mission—to your staff and then to the young people they serve.

## Goals and Objectives

*"My goal is to create an environment where kids can be around adults who give a damn."*

—DAVID DE LA FUENTE, director, High Point YMCA, Seattle, Washington

With a vision of healthy, productive young people; with a mission that motivates staff to emphasize people over activities; and with a philosophy that features the building of assets, people working in organizations that serve youth can then strive to formulate goals toward making the vision a reality. Earlier I showed you what Clackamas and Taylor Houses' philosophical orientations look like. Here's the next step, their goals:

1. To provide a safe and supportive environment for all clients and staff.
2. To create and implement individualized service plans for each youth based on *their* needs, strengths, and goals.
3. To prepare each youth for independent living and to succeed in wherever they will be living after they leave CH and TH.
4. Have staff serve as a constant role model within the facilities, the division, and throughout the Children's Federation.

You can see that the vision is continually being made more "real," more specific, as it flows through the mission, into the philosophy, and then on into the goals. When you read the goals of Clackamas and Taylor Houses, you get a sense of what people there are trying to *do*.

Here's a strong effort from the community of Dayton, Nevada. Along with "asset-building task forces" from nearby Fernley, Silver Springs, and Virginia City, they conducted interviews with members of local schools, the court system, and family advocates; reviewed the information; and "prioritized three risks and three assets on which to focus their time and energy." Based on those risks and assets, they formulated goals:

**Risks**

1. Substance use and abuse
2. Parent supports, including family management and favorable parental attitudes toward alcohol and drug use
3. Low commitment to school

**Assets**

1. Constructive use of time
2. Adult role models
3. Restraint and resistance skills

**Goals**

➤ Find out what kids and other adults are interested in and mobilize/create (but not staff) those opportunities as needed to succeed.

➤ Help develop more positive role models out of people in positions of power and influence and strengthen those who are positive role models.

➤ Create an opportunity/structure for youth to have a consistent and ongoing voice in town matters and in setting standards for their peers and adults in the community.

➤ Recruit more youth to get involved as peer leaders/asset builders to offer peer support groups and lead the way in changing cultural and social norms.

➤ Educate the public about the factors of use of alcohol and other drugs among young people. Publicize the positive about all ages!

➤ Create a resource place in the community to help students be prepared and be on equal footing as they enter and attend school (books, supplies, etc.).

The Dayton Asset-Building Task Force then chose to focus its resources on the following:

1. Sponsoring three Youth Corps members to work with younger children as reading buddies and to serve as Asset Ambassadors on committees and task forces, as well as organize a Passion Project that reflects their interests and that they can share with middle school students in their community.

2. [Running] a mentoring program using the developmental assets approach with 20 adult mentors and 20 student mentees 11–17 years of age who are involved in the juvenile justice system. Five of these mentors are high school youth who will serve as representatives of the "Stand Tall" teen organization dedicated to the prevention of underage drinking. They will mentor younger teens who are first-time offenders with substance abuse.

Again, observe the flow: from a vision through the mission and philosophy to the reduction of risks and promotion of assets and then to the goals and the eventual application of those goals. All this is from *A Millennium for Change: Creating Caring Communities in Lyon and Storey Counties That Are Healthy Places for Youth to Grow, Learn, and Live*—a "status report on the risks and assets of five communities in Storey and Lyon Counties." I like this approach because it brings together two schools of thought that many people think are diametrically opposed—risk reduction and asset building. Which way do you want to go? some have asked: Do you want to focus on problems, or do you want to focus on strengths? Let me tell it to you here: Reducing risks and building assets are complementary. They're not even two sides of the same coin, because unlike heads and tails, they can occur simultaneously. Think of them rather as the treble and bass to fine-tuned music.

Camp Fire USA has wholeheartedly adopted the developmental assets framework and integrated it into its goals. Deanna Armstrong, national director of programs, services, and expansion, reports that the goals of all the organization's K–5 curricula—"Starflight" for students in grades K–2 and "Adventure" for students in grades 3–5—are now tied to 14 specific assets they believe their programs help foster in youth. "This is exactly the direction we want to go," says Armstrong.

Here's another example—this one from the Teen Action Agenda of the Covington Family YMCA in Covington, Georgia, just outside Atlanta. This approach clearly links the goals of the program to the overall vision and mission of the organization:

**Goals**
➤ *Create a sense of unity, community, and belonging* for teens as members of a diverse and welcoming organization.

➤ *Develop assets* in teens, resulting in positive outcomes by enhancing teen health, education, and character development.

➤ *Build skills,* enabling teens to become successful adults, encouraging lifelong active citizenship through meaningful roles in their community.

➤ *Implement a community-wide initiative* by developing partnerships and combining community resources for the Teen Action Agenda.

**Objectives**

**1.** Leadership and Service Learning *(Spirit)*

**1.1** Help teens plan and implement community projects.

**1.2** Link teens with younger children, serving as role models, mentors, and tutors.

**1.3** Connect teens with older adults, sharing friendships, insight, experience, and mutual support.

**1.4** Involve teens as YMCA volunteers in programs, events, and activities of all kinds.

**1.5** Provide teens with service learning opportunities within the community.

**1.6** Offer teens meaningful roles to serve on YMCA boards, committees, task forces, and focus groups.

**2.** Education, Career, and Life Skills *(Mind)*

**2.1** Encourage academic success by providing mentoring and tutoring programs.

**2.2** Offer special programs for at-risk youth.

**2.3** Implement a *Life Skills Training* curriculum that will serve as a model for community programs.

**2.4** Help teens set and achieve career goals through internships, apprenticeships, and shadowing programs.

**2.5** Develop money management skills.

**3.** Health, Safety, and Well-Being *(Body)*

**3.1** Promote healthy lifestyles through health, fitness, wellness, and sports programs.

**3.2** Help teens avoid substance abuse, HIV infection, pregnancy, gangs, and violence.

**3.3** Provide assistance with health care needs.

**3.4** Develop a Teen Resource Referral system.

**4.** Teen-Centered Recreation, Programs, and Activities *(Fun)*

**4.1** Create a Teen Council.

**4.2** Develop and fund a Teen Activity Center.

**4.3** Design, fund, and implement a *Weekends Program* for teens.

And from the YMCA of Greater Seattle:

Since its founding in 1844, the mission of the YMCA has been to affirm the positive values by which lives of character and purpose can be lived. Central to this work has been the YMCA's regard for youth as a resource in building vital communities.

The goal of YMCA youth development programs is to provide *all* young people opportunities to participate in and contribute toward the improvement of their communities.

*The YMCA is a movement of young persons committed to serving others.*

**Objectives**

1. **To recruit young people**—especially those unable to realize their potential due to lack of opportunity—to participate in diverse, age-appropriate activities;

2. **To surround young people**—with strong positive examples of responsible adult role models of the highest character and skill;

3. **To engage young people**—in contributing to their communities, with special emphasis on mobilizing the unique gifts of energy and moral idealism that young people possess; and

4. **To infuse common good values**—respect, responsibility, honesty, caring, faith, and fun, through experiences that lead to a life-long commitment to service in the community.

All YMCA programs—from swimming lessons to leaders clubs, childcare to camping—will be provided and evaluated in light of this goal and these objectives.

The Eau Claire Coalition for Youth, in Eau Claire, Wisconsin, explicitly incorporates assets into its goals:

➤ To assist in engaging the schools, families, community organizations/agencies, and local congregations of Eau Claire to work together to promote assets in the youth they have contact with daily.

➤ To give youth the direction and specific resources to get things done.

➤ To break down any barriers between youth due to their specific race, creed, or school so that together assets can increase and unhealthy behaviors will disappear.

Holly Rutherford-Allen is the manager of annual giving for the Girl Scouts-Mile Hi Council in Denver. The Mile Hi Council has infused developmental assets into its Girl Scout Program Goals. Here are some examples:

**Girl Scouting Program Goal 1**—Develop to her full individual potential.

[Assets: Personal power, Self-esteem, Sense of purpose, Positive view of personal future.]

**Girl Scouting Program Goal 2**—Relate to others with increasing understanding, skill, and respect.

[Assets: Equality and social justice, Interpersonal competence, Cultural competence, Positive peer influence, Peaceful conflict resolution.]

**Girl Scouting Program Goal 3**—Develop values to guide her actions and to improve the foundation for sound decision making.

[Assets: Caring, Integrity, Honesty, Responsibility, Restraint, Resistance skills.]

**Girl Scouting Program Goal 4**—Contribute to the improvement of society through the use of her abilities and leadership skills, working in cooperation with others.

[Assets: Community values youth, Youth as resources, Service to others.]

Now that's fine as far as it goes. But can it go deeper? It still seems as if we have two decks of cards: One deck is all the organization's activities—what it does, what the young people do. The other deck is the developmental assets. How can we shuffle these two decks together so that the organization's activities are tied to the assets, so that people understand that when they're doing *this activity*, then they're promoting *this asset*?

The Mile Hi Council has shuffled the decks together: It has linked every "Try-It" activity for Brownie Girl Scouts, every Badge for Junior Girl Scouts, and every "Interest Project" for Cadette and Senior Girl Scouts to developmental assets. Thus, the council ensures that virtually all the youth programs and activities in the organization provide girls with the opportunity to build specific developmental assets.

In the "Try-It" called "All in the Family," Brownie Girl Scouts:

➤ Share a photograph of their family as well as a family story, tradition, dance, or type of food with others in their troop.

➤ Put on a "Family Night" art show and invite the families of everyone the troop to the exhibit.

➤ Make a family time capsule.

➤ Plan healthy family meals, go on a family run, or participate in some other fitness activity.

Assets promoted: Family support, Positive family communication, Other adult relationships, High expectations, Creative activities, Youth programs, Achievement motivation, and Planning and decision making.

In the "Badge" called "Becoming a Teen," Junior Girl Scouts:

➤ Find out about girls in their teens who have achieved success and analyze why they were successful.

➤ Read a book with a teenage girl as the main character and organize a book swap.

➤ Set up a personal care schedule and follow it.

➤ Interview two or more teenage girls to understand how they handle an increased amount of freedom and responsibility that comes with getting older.

➤ Analyze the accuracy of how girls and boys are depicted in magazines, books, and television.

➤ Interview family members to find out what it was like for them when they were teenagers.

➤ Plan a coming-of-age ceremony with a group of friends.

Assets promoted: Positive family communication, Other adult relationships, High expectations, Youth programs, Achievement motivation, Personal power.

In the "Interest Project" called "On a High Note," Cadettes and Senior Girl Scouts:

➤ Take a poll in their class or troop about the most popular types of music and plan a musical program that includes those types.

➤ Plan a karaoke party for their troop.

➤ Visit a variety of places of worship and discuss with their troop how different faiths listened to similar or different types of music.

➤ Attend at least three different types of musical performances and keep a journal about their experiences.

➤ Visit a music store to discover which instruments rely on computer technology.

➤ Visit a museum and create a scrapbook about the changes that instruments have undergone.

➤ Plan a singing show at a local nursing home.

➤ Work with younger girls to create their own band using both handmade and school-band instruments.

➤ Explore different musical careers.

➤ Write a poem and collaborate with someone to put it to music.

➤ Practice being disc jockeys and create a half-hour musical program.

Assets promoted: Other adult relationships, Youth as resources, Service to others, High expectations, Creative activities, Youth programs, Religious community, Achievement motivation, Cultural competence.

Virtually everything the Girl Scouts do is associated with a developmental asset. What makes this work is not just the linkages. Rutherford-Allen also has troop leaders discuss with the Scouts which assets they need; the results of those discussions then become the guides for the girls' activities.

Most organizations serving youth already have goals that are probably unimpeachable. I cited the previous examples to show you how incorporating the asset framework into your organization's goals adds a dimension to whatever activities you end up doing. That dimension is *intentionality*. With the framework in place and the goals determining the direction, your activities become more focused on young people's strengths and your efforts become more focused on building relationships.

*How closely are the goals and objectives of your organization tied to the organization's vision, mission, and philosophy?*

*How closely are they tied to developmental assets?*

*Do the objectives and activities of your organization flow directly from the goals?*

*Are people throughout the organization clear about both the "little picture" of activities as well as the "big picture" of vision, mission, philosophy, and goals and objectives?*

# Staffing

*"It's all about the people, and how they interact with children."*

—SUZANNE FIELDING, executive director,

New Mexico Council of Camp Fire USA

Rick Jackson "gets it." When he was vice president of the YMCA of Greater Seattle, Jackson would customarily lead off a presentation to executive leaders not by reeling off statistics about whom the Y had served and what activities the Y had completed the past year but by asking the participants who was there for them when they were growing up. Which adults made a difference in your life? he would ask. Who listened to you? Who helped you to participate, to take risks, to make a difference? Jackson would use the ensuing, typically earnest discussions as a gauge to measure the success of the Y. For the participants would describe individuals and situations in the way Jackson wanted to base the environment and staff at the YMCA.

Even now the YMCA of Greater Seattle routinely asks its staff, How are you making a difference in the lives of youth? The responses serve several purposes:

➤ They give people an opportunity to acknowledge their own good work;

➤ They serve as models for everyone else;

➤ They're evidence for how the organization is helping young people build assets; and

➤ They make people feel good.

Here's a response from Lisa Windle:

In addition to working with the YMCA, I also coach cross-country and track and field at Cedarcrest High School. Over the past seven years, I have developed a coaching style that goes beyond the technical aspects of the sport:

➤ Athletes are encouraged to participate in the development of their training.

➤ Athletes are encouraged to act as "models" for younger athletes coming into the program.

➤ Our team is a "community." We are all responsible for its success, safety, etc.

> ➤ Education is a value and athletes participate as "tutorees" and "tutors."
> ➤ My role is to better motivate their mind, body, and spirit.

And here's another response that testifies to the power of a staff person. This is from Administrative Assistant Danielle Rowland:

I work in the Association Office, where we can feel somewhat removed from the life-changing work that's done at the program level. Recently, however, I had a conversation with one of my housemates that made me feel less removed. Entering her first year of teaching at Aki Kurose Middle School Academy, she was feeling a little overwhelmed with all the work to be done just to prepare. She came home from her first official prep day exclaiming, "The Y people at my school are so cool. Today I met Lon Zell Hill and Sprout Hochberg. Have you met them? They're amazing! I just have to say that the teachers at my school *love* having the Y there. Whenever there's extra stuff that we need help with, they're always willing to help."

After the school year was under way, she mentioned them again. "Lon Zell and Sprout always walk the halls, helping kids get to their classes, helping to maintain a positive environment in the school. I'm not sure what their job description is. I think they're just in charge of setting up the after-school program. But they go beyond what other groups do—beyond what I would expect in terms of support. They seem to care as much about making Aki Kurose a great school as the teachers do. Lon Zell is really a good role model for my kids. It's been helpful to have his influence in my classroom, and in the school in general. The kids really love and respect him.

"Sprout is always cheerful and takes a lot of relational initiative. One day she just came up to me in the lunchroom and asked me how things were going with my classes and how I was doing. I really appreciated that. Another time, a student's mom came into the school and when I asked her if I could help her, she replied, 'Do you have a program called Sprout?' I asked, 'Do you mean the YMCA?' It took a minute to convince her that Sprout wasn't the program. Obviously, her child had had some significant interactions with Sprout!"

Hearing these things from my housemate has made me feel proud to work for the YMCA and thankful that people like Lon Zell and Sprout give so much of themselves to their work.

That's the power of one staff person to contribute to an asset-rich environment.

Suzanne Fielding recognizes that the most asset-rich vision, mission, philosophy, and goals won't affect a single individual if the people entrusted to the care of youth don't know how to relate to them in asset-rich ways. Read the following excerpt from Fielding's 2001 *KIDS CARE Training Manual,* and think about how you and the people you work with might answer the questions:

> What we are talking about here is at the very heart of any school-age program. If staff responds to children sensitively, you will have the main ingredient for a great program. If the emotional environment is one of acceptance and understanding for children, families, and staff, the program will be a positive experience for everyone. These questions will help you to check on the emotional climate of your program:
>
> ➤ Do the staff make children feel welcome and treat them with respect? Are staff compassionate about children's many feelings? Do staff have the time to talk with individual children and get to know each child's interests, abilities, and talents? Are staff culturally responsive?
>
> ➤ Are staff actively involved with children? Do they work with the children every day to build positive relationships and model communication? Do they help children make informed and responsible decisions? Do staff have realistic expectations of children? Do staff help children without taking control?
>
> ➤ Do staff model cooperation and respect? Do staff set appropriate limits for children? Do they help children learn how to solve their conflicts? Do the children cooperate and show respect for each other?
>
> ➤ Are families welcome at the program and do they feel well informed? Do the staff and families work together to make this a positive experience for the children? Are the diverse needs of families recognized and viewed as strengths? Are staff responsive to issues affecting the children's lives outside the program?

At the core of creating asset-rich environments are people—usually but not always staff—walking their talk. That's what Paul Vidas does.

That's what Ivory Smith does. And that's what Sylvia Bastidos does, too. "Silve" facilitates a Reading Circle in El Paso for Hispanic teenagers. She introduces a book, reads it with them, and leads a discussion about how the characters in the book have reflected developmental assets. The teenagers then talk about how to implement specific assets in their own lives. But the interesting—and asset-rich—component of this interaction is not the reading circle itself; it's that Silve, decades past her teen years, speaks very broken English. What a great message! "If I can learn to speak and read English, you certainly can." How could her students possibly say it's too difficult and give up in the face of such a model?

### Rethinking Roles

Rick Jackson has worked tirelessly to effect systemic change in the way we view young people. He offers some new "job descriptions" that are more consistent with building assets than traditional job descriptions. For example, here is Jackson's new description for "youth worker":

> ➤ Excellent in working with youth *and* in a "community development approach" to youth development—"on fire" with purpose and possibilities.
> ➤ Must be able to build bridges between youth and adults, and form intergenerational teams to do the community's work.
> ➤ Creative in recruiting volunteers: college students, young adults, and other caring adults; great at asking for what is needed, and saying "thanks."

If you're a youth worker, I can almost hear you saying, "Hey, I can't be in this alone. I just don't have time to mentor every kid I meet." Research bears you out. For example, a recent study by the Indiana Youth Institute (*Youth Work: More Than Child's Play;* 1999) found that most "front line" youth workers have more on their plates than building relationships: things like budgets, paperwork, and fund-raising. The study also found that youth workers report the following as the most frustrating aspects of their jobs:
> ➤ Lack of resources;
> ➤ Low salaries and benefits;
> ➤ Lack of parental support; and
> ➤ Agency bureaucracy

And if you're like the youth workers surveyed in the Indiana Youth Institute study, what helps you persist despite these frustrations are the opportunities to make a difference in the lives of the young people you're working with.

The good news is that you're not alone—or at least you shouldn't be. Jackson also rethought the roles of other people involved with organizations that serve youth—executives, board members, heads of foundations, and funders:

**Top Management:**

➤ Read systems theory and the science of complexity—it offers some good advice for running your agency/business today. It's the way young people think—some of the time.

➤ Get out of the rut of narrow organizational "problem solving" and "strategic planning"—the world is much too dynamic for those tools alone.

➤ Ask the question[s], "Who else cares about positive youth development in this town?" [and] "Have I spoken to or listened to them lately?"

➤ LEAD by asking your board members good youth development questions.

➤ Convene meetings across institutions—nonprofit, private, public.

**Board Member:**

➤ Help your organization maintain the Big Picture and the Long View regarding positive youth development.

➤ Don't be overly swayed by big numbers or dramatic turnaround stories.

➤ Remember that the work of building assets in youth is an everyday job, that positive outcomes grow in small increments over many years.

➤ Always ask the questions, "Why is this program working?" and "Which assets does this activity build?"

**Foundation Executive:**

➤ Stop funding "programs."

➤ Start funding innovation and innovators, especially when intergenerational.

➤ Ask questions, face-to-face, with youth and youth workers, about what would help build assets.

➤ Take the long view (no more one-year grants).

➤ Fund cross-institutional partnerships for five-year periods; create incentives for collaboration.

➤ Remember that philanthropy is more about caring than about cash. Insist that others remember it, too.

**Government Funder:**

➤ (see above, "Foundation Executive")

➤ As citizens, we have the added responsibility to support good public policies, which provide needed community services and supports for youth and families.

➤ Insist service "providers" view their work in the context of asset building and link with other institutions in the community.

Of course, these job descriptions are only the beginning. Think about this for a moment: If the focus is no longer the activity but the young person, then there are a lot more people who can potentially affect that young person than just the activity director. To that end, YMCA of Greater Seattle President and CEO Neil Nicoll trains his entire staff— including custodians, receptionists, and secretaries—in the asset framework, because they're all in positions to make positive changes in young people's lives. And on the receiving end, Jenifer Gauthier—also with the YMCA of Greater Seattle—emphasizes in her trainings that staff should be building assets with all young people they see, not just the ones who come to the Y.

**Hiring**

As I mentioned earlier, members of Seattle's Promoting Assets Across Cultures Team have chosen their own coordinator using their own criteria: What is the applicant's experience with youth? What is the applicant's potential to forge good relationships? And how would the applicant respond to a variety of tough situations, for example, fights or child abuse? The young people leading the Mosaic Youth Center in metropolitan Minneapolis also select their own coordinator, with help from adults in the organization. Having youth choose their coordinators is an excellent and practical way to ensure that people connect with the young people they serve. Another way is to hire youth who come up through the ranks as junior staff or in other leadership roles. (In their 1994 study of neighborhood organizations in which youth thrive—*Urban Sanctuaries: Neighborhood Organizations in the Lives and Futures of Inner-City Youth*—Milbrey McLaughlin and her colleagues found this practice to be quite common.) David Foster, youth services director at the McGaw YMCA in Evanston, Illinois, believes that the most important qualification for potential staff is their ability to connect with young people. That sentiment is shared by New Mexico Council of Camp Fire USA Executive Director Suzanne Fielding, quoted at the beginning of this section. For her that means, in part, recruiting staff from school communities and hiring many stay-at-home mothers who are ready to reenter the work force.

The hiring and training of staff are critical components in building assets with youth. If the original vision of the organization is to filter down into behaviors that support young people, then everyone needs to be "on board," "with the program"—walking their talk. Carol White of the Tillamook County Family YMCA in Oregon prepares her staff with formal guidelines and expectations—for how the staff interact with children, how they interact with each other, how the physical environment should support the children, how the program should link with families and the community. You can do the same thing in your organization: You can set out guidelines and expectations based on the developmental assets and use them to anchor the staff to the asset framework. Figure 3.2 provides an example of one way you might do this.

You can also use the framework (and perhaps a chart similar to the one in Figure 3.2) as a tool for hiring ("How would you help build each asset?"), for program building ("How can we do more to help build these specific assets?"), or for staff evaluation ("How can you improve on your efforts to help build these assets?"). Remember, as part of a youth-serving organization, you may not be in a position to affect every one of the 40 assets; and in any case, you may not have the support to do that. But I've included all the assets in the sample chart to show you how much might enter into staff orientation and training within the asset framework. In most cases the framework isn't antagonistic to what you're already doing; it just offers a structure by which you can more easily understand and put into action what you want to do. In the case of the Tillamook County Family YMCA, Carol White gets support for the asset framework at the

## Figure 3.2

## Asset-Building Plan

Staff member: _____

Position: _____ Date: _____

| Developmental Asset | How I Regularly Help Young People Build It | Effective Strategies I Can Share with Colleagues | Something New I'll Try |
|---|---|---|---|
| SUPPORT | | | |
| 1. **Family support—** Family life provides high levels of love and support. | | | |
| 2. **Positive family communication—**Young person and her or his parent(s) communicate positively, and young person is willing to seek advice and counsel from parent(s). | | | |
| 3. **Other adult relationships—**Young person receives support from three or more nonparent adults. | | | |
| 4. **Caring neighborhood—**Young person experiences caring neighbors. | | | |
| 5. **Caring school climate**—School provides a caring, encouraging environment. | | | |
| 6. **Parent involvement in schooling—**Parent(s) are actively involved in helping young person succeed in school. | | | |

| Developmental Asset | How I Regularly Help Young People Build It | Effective Strategies I Can Share with Colleagues | Something New I'll Try |
|---|---|---|---|
| **EMPOWERMENT** | | | |
| **7. Community values youth**—Young person perceives that adults in the community value youth. | | | |
| **8. Youth as resources**—Young people are given useful roles in the community. | | | |
| **9. Service to others**—Young person serves in the community one hour or more per week. | | | |
| **10. Safety**—Young person feels safe at home, at school, and in the neighborhood. | | | |
| **BOUNDARIES AND EXPECTATIONS** | | | |
| **11. Family boundaries**—Family has clear rules and consequences and monitors the young person's whereabouts. | | | |
| **12. School boundaries**—School provides clear rules and consequences. | | | |
| **13. Neighborhood boundaries**—Neighbors take responsibility for monitoring young people's behavior. | | | |

| Developmental Asset | How I Regularly Help Young People Build It | Effective Strategies I Can Share with Colleagues | Something New I'll Try |
|---|---|---|---|
| **14. Adult role models**— Parent(s) and other adults model positive, responsible behavior. | | | |
| **15. Positive peer influence**—Young person's best friends model responsible behavior. | | | |
| **16. High expectations**— Both parent(s) and teachers encourage the young person to do well. | | | |
| CONSTRUCTIVE USE OF TIME | | | |
| **17. Creative activities**— Young person spends three or more hours per week in lessons or practice in music, theater, or other arts. | | | |
| **18. Youth programs**— Young person spends three or more hours per week in sports, clubs, or organizations at school and/or in the community. | | | |
| **19. Religious community**— Young person spends one or more hours per week in activities in a religious institution. | | | |
| **20. Time at home**—Young person is out with friends "with nothing special to do" two or fewer nights per week. | | | |

| Developmental Asset | How I Regularly Help Young People Build It | Effective Strategies I Can Share with Colleagues | Something New I'll Try |
|---|---|---|---|
| **COMMITMENT TO LEARNING** | | | |
| **21. Achievement motivation**—Young person is motivated to do well in school. | | | |
| **22. School engagement**—Young person is actively engaged in learning. | | | |
| **23. Homework**—Young person reports doing at least one hour of homework every school day. | | | |
| **24. Bonding to school**—Young person cares about her or his school. | | | |
| **25. Reading for pleasure**—Young person reads for pleasure three or more hours per week. | | | |
| **POSITIVE VALUES** | | | |
| **26. Caring**—Young person places high value on helping other people. | | | |
| **27. Equality and social justice**—Young person places high value on promoting equality and reducing hunger and poverty. | | | |

| Developmental Asset | How I Regularly Help Young People Build It | Effective Strategies I Can Share with Colleagues | Something New I'll Try |
|---|---|---|---|
| 28. **Integrity**—Young person acts on convictions and stands up for her or his beliefs. | | | |
| 29. **Honesty**—Young person "tells the truth even when it is not easy." | | | |
| 30. **Responsibility**—Young person accepts and takes personal responsibility. | | | |
| 31. **Restraint**—Young person believes it is important not to be sexually active or to use alcohol or other drugs. | | | |
| SOCIAL COMPETENCIES | | | |
| 32. **Planning and decision making**—Young person knows how to plan ahead and make choices. | | | |
| 33. **Interpersonal competence**—Young person has empathy, sensitivity, and friendship skills. | | | |
| 34. **Cultural competence**—Young person has knowledge of and comfort with people of different cultural/racial/ethnic backgrounds. | | | |

| Developmental Asset | How I Regularly Help Young People Build It | Effective Strategies I Can Share with Colleagues | Something New I'll Try |
|---|---|---|---|
| **35. Resistance skills—** Young person can resist negative peer pressure and dangerous situations. | | | |
| **36. Peaceful conflict resolution—** Young person seeks to resolve conflict nonviolently. | | | |
| POSITIVE IDENTITY | | | |
| **37. Personal power—** Young person feels he or she has control over "things that happen to me." | | | |
| **38. Self-esteem—** Young person reports having a high self-esteem. | | | |
| **39. Sense of purpose—** Young person reports that "my life has a purpose." | | | |
| **40. Positive view of personal future—** Young person is optimistic about her or his personal future. | | | |

administrative level. Executive Director Mike Ellis has his directors analyze their programs and figure out what opportunities they had to build assets—what they're doing now, how they can improve, and what tools they need.

## Support

No matter how employees are chosen, they probably won't stay around too long if they don't receive support from their supervisors; and if they do stay around, they probably won't be very happy. The McGaw YMCA's David Foster tries to model building assets with his staff—not expecting perfection right away, but nurturing people and giving them opportunities to succeed. At one point he was about to fire someone, but then recalled that when *he* began his career, he gave his supervisor many opportunities to get rid of him. His supervisor had told Foster, however, that he saw tremendous potential in him and thought that if he kept working with him, someday he'd realize all that he had to offer the YMCA. So Foster was thinking of how he had benefited from mentoring and arranged for *his* employee to be mentored. Happy ending: According to Foster, the staff person "turned around completely."

When Heidi Struve-Harvey of the Washoe County Department of Juvenile Services in Reno, Nevada, trains her staff, they review each age group of young people, discuss what's going on in those age groups developmentally and socially, and then determine how to build assets for that population. Tina Martinez, director of programs at the Boys and Girls Clubs of Metro Denver, includes discussions of the asset framework in every orientation for new employees and volunteers.

Sound Youth AmeriCorps works with schools, congregations, community agencies, and neighborhood volunteers in the greater Seattle area to build assets. They place AmeriCorps members to work directly with children and youth and to recruit volunteers for tutoring and out-of-school enrichment programs in low-income communities. Their training is extensive; the following excerpt from their "Getting Things Done" program narrative exemplifies a supportive environment for staff. See how it compares with what you're doing in your organization:

> [Our] training schedule begins with a two-week orientation. This orientation includes informational sessions on the Corporation for National Service and the developmental assets model. When we have

successfully described what Sound Youth is . . . then we are able to teach the skills our members need to meet our vision and objectives. We offer intensive, age-appropriate tutor trainings. In these, members learn the basics of tutoring children and youth in literacy and numeracy skills. We also provide trainings in program planning and implementation. Step by step, members learn how to create healthy, appropriate, and dynamic youth programs.

At the beginning of the second week, members spend two days becoming oriented to their sites. At their sites, they get to know their colleagues, become clear in their site-specific expectations, and become familiar with the communities in which they serve. After they have a clear picture of their service, the Sound Youth team goes on a three-day team-building and goal-setting retreat. We take the challenge of low and high ropes courses, take a skills inventory of the group, and set community goals and individual goals.

We continue the skill and community building by gathering for six-hour Friday meetings. More specific skill training in conflict resolution, working with immigrant populations, tutoring children who have learning disabilities, mentoring diverse populations, and positive discipline take half the day. The trainings are determined by Sound Youth staff for the first half of the year and by members in the second half. Starting in February, trainings are determined by our entire team through a consensus-building process.

Our weekly meetings are also composed of check-in/trouble-shooting sessions. Members bring challenges they face to the table, and as a team we work to help each other resolve conflicts and face challenges. These sessions enable all of us to become very familiar with the others' sites and [with] the community at large.

Members also serve on Sound Youth committees. There are three committees: newsletter, social health, and service project. Each member serves on one committee throughout the year. This promotes leadership in each member of our team. The committees meet during Friday meetings.

Lastly, members share their talents during our Fridays. Our talent sharing allows us to know what skills lie in our group as well as help to build respect among our members. Hidden talents arise, and we all leave with a little piece of information or skill that we can bring back to our day-to-day service.

The last component to our training schedule is retreats. In addition to our retreat during orientation, we go on a rejuvenation, renewal retreat in March, and a celebratory, reflective retreat in July. The retreats are planned collaboratively by members and staff. They often include workshops conceived of and implemented by members.

### Recognition

Part of support is honoring the good things people do, especially when they go beyond what's expected. I quoted from the *KIDS CARE* manual used by the New Mexico Council of Camp Fire USA when I was discussing how relationships between staff and young people benefit young people. The KIDS CARE program cares about its staff, too. One of the things they do to recognize outstanding efforts is to give "Outstanding Achievement Awards" that honor employees for one or more of the following:

➤ Providing a positive role model for the children.

➤ Promoting self-esteem and self-reliance in all children.

➤ Projecting Camp Fire's professionalism and positive philosophy to all parents, children, staff, host personnel, and the community.

➤ Enthusiasm and support of Camp Fire's goals, objectives, and programming.

➤ Instilling in the children a concern for others and our environment.

➤ Encouraging volunteerism in the community by the children in the program.

➤ Fulfilling all job requirements with high standards.

➤ Displaying flexibility, cooperation, and a positive attitude.

➤ A singular outstanding act.

This is walking your talk on a different level. You want staff to acknowledge young people for their achievements, and for the same reasons you should want to acknowledge staff for *their* achievements.

The Eau Claire Coalition for Youth calls its version of an Outstanding Achievement Award the "Asset Builder of the Month." Here's how the coalition notifies nominees:

Congratulations! You have been nominated by the Eau Claire Community Asset Building Committee to be our "Asset Builder of the Month"! Your work with youth is admired by many in our community, and we would like to show you our appreciation by having you featured in the "Building Up Kids" section of the *Leader-Telegram*. The feature will be in one of the upcoming "Parenting" sections, which is included only in Thursday's newspaper.

Would you be so kind to fill out the enclosed information form as soon as possible and return it in the self-addressed envelope? Secondly, we will need a picture of you for the feature! You can either enclose a black-and-white or color photo of yourself or stop in . . . and get your picture taken.

The "Asset Builder of the Month" form asks nominees to list the activities they're involved in with youth as well as to state the main reason for their both working with youth and developing assets in them. The Eau Claire Coalition for Youth simultaneously acknowledges and motivates people working to build assets by asking them to sign this commitment statement:

*Do all the people in your organization feel that they are making a positive difference in the lives of youth?*

> As a result of this . . . public event, I intend to continue the asset building with youth to make changes in the lives of young people so that they lead happier, healthier, and more successful lives.

*Do their job descriptions and everyday responsibilities give them the opportunities to do that?*

They even give people "pledges" to fill out and keep as a reminder of that commitment:

*What are the criteria for hiring staff in your organization?*

> I pledge to continue being an "Asset Builder" to help make a positive difference in my life and in the lives of other youth and adults in the Eau Claire community. I will take the following steps . . .

*What's important for staff to know about your organization?*

Just as teachers are possibly the most important component of young people's education, so staff are possibly the most important component of young people's experiences in organizations. They are the ones who interact directly with young people; they are the ones who model behaviors—positive as well as negative. Ensuring that staff are uniformly communicating—explicitly and implicitly—positive, asset-building messages to youth is absolutely necessary.

*How are staff in your organization supported?*

*How are staff in your organization recognized and rewarded?*

# Monitoring Progress

*Sound Youth will use the developmental assets as our guide in monitoring our project. We have used the developmental asset categories of Commitment to Learning and Social Competencies as guides to craft our objectives. We will use the assets within the two categories as our measurable indicators.*

—"GETTING THINGS DONE," Sound Youth, Seattle, Washington

Finally, from the administrator's perspective, let's talk about monitoring progress. Sometimes it's difficult to gauge how well you're doing something. Not every tree bears fruit in one season. And, to continue the metaphor, it's sometimes tough to agree on what an outstanding piece of fruit should look, feel, and taste like. Finally, it often takes more money to assess the fruit than it did to plant and cultivate the tree.

Nonetheless, you don't want to plant weeds. You want to continue your successes and avoid your mistakes. You want to have information about what you did and how you did it. Just because it isn't easy doesn't mean you shouldn't do it. After all, isn't that what you'd tell the young people in your organization?

While no single, formal, standardized process or tool exists to measure the effectiveness of building developmental assets (outcome), nor is there a formal, standardized tool to monitor the extent to which staff, for example, are *trying* to help build assets (process), there are several tools from Search Institute that can be of assistance. They include *What's Working? Tools for Evaluating Your Mentoring Program, Making the Case: Measuring the Impact of Youth Development Programs* (a report with ideas and suggestions for program evaluation), and *First Steps in Evaluation: Basic Tools for Asset-Building Initiatives.* Or, as others have, you can devise measures on your own that give you feedback on both counts. You can monitor how well staff are adhering to the asset framework, and you can get a rough idea of what happens as a result.

One approach is to develop an oversight committee and include monitoring progress as one of the group's responsibilities. Oversight committees can take different forms, but take note of the one described in the following information from the YMCA of Metro Atlanta. I want to draw your attention to the formal and somewhat bureaucratic language—not to criticize it, but to acknowledge it. You know you've arrived when what you do is described in such a manner. In many cases, this is what it means to be accepted into the system. And, make no mistake about it, it's good to be accepted into the system. That's when the norms have changed; that's when the developmental assets model has become the norm. And that's what you should be aiming for.

### General Commission

The Asset Development Oversight Committee is commissioned on behalf of the Board of Directors to position the Metro Atlanta YMCA and its collaborators as a key catalyst in increasing the asset development capacity of the citizens of the Greater Metropolitan Atlanta area and for raising the public consciousness about the urgency and feasibility of mobilizing individuals, communities, policymakers, and resources to take positive action on behalf of all children and adolescents.

### Composition

The Chairperson of the Board of the Metropolitan Atlanta YMCA will appoint the Chair of the Asset Development Oversight Committee and approve the selection of committee members. The Group Vice President for Membership will serve as staff liaison to the committee. Meetings will be called twice a year. (Specially called meetings may be added.)

### Duties of the Committee

1. Provide leadership for the design and selection of a metro-wide, multi-sector, Asset Development Oversight Committee.
2. Receive, review, and approve the recommendations of the Metro Atlanta YMCA Asset Development Model Implementation Committee.
3. Provide input, counseling, and feedback on the metro-wide integration of Search Institute's asset development framework into the daily operations, staff development, volunteer development, and all membership and program delivery areas of the collaborators.
4. Monitor and evaluate the effectiveness of the Metro Atlanta YMCA and its collaborators as an asset-building coalition and as a social change agent within the greater Metro Atlanta area with regard to increasing overall asset development capacity.
5. Leverage public policy, public and private funding, and

multi-sector collaboration opportunities to increase the long-term sustainability of a metro-wide asset awareness and development campaign.

The Asset Development Oversight Committee will give semi-annual reports to the Metro Board.

Regardless of who does the work of actually gathering information, there are a number of approaches to consider, depending on your needs, interests, resources, and program specifics. Seattle's Sound Youth Ameri-Corps measures progress using the following methods:

- ➤ Pre/post asset-based surveys distributed to youth;
- ➤ Members' monthly progress reports;
- ➤ Members' weekly meeting and check-in reports;
- ➤ Monthly site visits by Sound Youth staff;
- ➤ Semiannual progress reports and evaluations by site supervisors;
- ➤ Teacher interviews; and
- ➤ Student interviews.

Here are the main questions from a survey that Sound Youth Ameri-Corps has used to gather feedback from young people:

We need your help so that we can learn more about you and our program. It would be great if you would take a few minutes to answer the questions on this survey. You are not required to do this—it is completely up to you. Your answers will not affect your grades or be shared with your teacher or your parents. THANKS!

**Section 1.**

INSTRUCTIONS: For each statement below, color in the SUN if your answer is YES or color in the CLOUD if your answer is NO.

1. I have friends in my class.
2. When I have a disagreement with a friend, I think it is best to keep my feelings to myself.
3. I have a hard time making decisions.
4. When friends try to make me do something I don't want to do, I can say "NO!"

5. Most of the time, school is a fun place to be.

6. When I have a problem with a friend, most of the time I can solve it by talking to them.

7. I have a friend my own age that I can talk to if I have a problem.

8. I think it is important to treat people nicely even if they are different than me.

9. I think it is important to do well in school.

10. When one of my friends is sad, I try to make them feel better.

11. It is easy to make decisions about what I want to do.

12. I enjoy learning about kids in my class who come from other parts of the world.

13. I like reading books with my family.

**Section 2.**

INSTRUCTIONS: Read the following statements and circle [a full-color flower] for ALL OF THE TIME, circle [a partially colored flower] for SOME OF THE TIME, and circle [a blank flower] for NEVER.

14. I am good at getting along with other kids in my school.

15. I care about other people's feelings.

16. I enjoy reading books.

17. I stand up for my beliefs.

18. I have to rush to get my homework done in time for school.

19. I tell the truth, even when it is not easy.

20. I try to do my best in school.

21. When I have free time, I read books.

22. When I am at school, I would rather be somewhere else.

23. I feel comfortable playing with kids who speak a different language than me.

24. I turn in school assignments on time.

25. When I have a problem with a friend, I talk to them about my feelings.

26. I need help making decisions.

27. When I wake up in the morning, I am excited to go to school.

The feedback from a survey can help you to fine-tune your program—to capitalize on your strengths and pinpoint and address your weaknesses.

Because the staff is usually the closest to and the most knowledge-able about what your organization is intending to do and what it actu-ally is doing, it makes sense to gather feedback from them regularly. It has often struck me that many organizations—youth-serving and oth-erwise—run two programs: the one on paper and the real one. Bringing staff into the decision-making process as well as providing opportunities for them to bridge the gap between those two programs is just good man-agement. Here's an example of a checklist for staff from Seattle's *It's About Time for Kids Asset-Building Manual*. Staff are asked to check yes, no, or not sure in response to each of the following questions:

1. Have you generated a strength-based initial interview form?
2. Do you use a strength-based planning methodology (i.e., perform extensive strengths, values, and preferences assess-ment, identify needs, *and* propose solutions that are based on child/family strengths, values, and preferences)?
3. Do you identify who the child/family turns to during times of stress or crisis?
4. Do parents/children have the opportunity to voice their own needs regardless of services that are currently available?
5. Do parents help evaluate the effectiveness of interventions for their children?
6. Are internal staffings or consultations required to begin with a presentation of the person's strengths?
7. Do you assist families with life plans, not treatment plans?
8. Do plans go beyond solving problems to create a life at least as good [as those of] other children and families in the community?
9. Do you work with parents as partners rather than serving as an expert?
10. Are plans created with representation of persons with similar cultural background as the family?
11. Do children/parents feel that their plans are theirs, not yours?
12. Do you have access to flexible funds in a high percentage of cases so the children/family can obtain what they need, not just what is available?
13. Do your child/family plan teams include at least 50 percent non-professionals with access to informal resources for the

family (family friends, relatives, neighbors, religious leaders, coaches, etc.)?

14. Do at least 50 percent of the plans for children/families involve informal and community resources?

15. Do at least 50 percent of the plans for children/families provide an opportunity for them to give back to others or the community?

16. Do you measure strength- or asset-based outcomes, not just reduction of problems?

Here are some survey questions developed by Search Institute and the YMCA of the USA and adapted by the YMCA of Middle Tennessee:

[Response options for the following questions are strongly agree, agree, disagree, strongly disagree.]

**Outcome #1: Provide a caring, supportive environment**

YMCA staff really care about me.

I would feel comfortable going to a staff person for advice if I had a serious problem.

I have a sense of belonging when I work with staff.

**Outcome #2: Help develop a sense of self**

Being involved in these activities, I feel like I can make a difference.

Staff expect that I give my best in all activities.

Staff challenge me to do my best.

There are clear rules about what I can and cannot do.

These activities have helped me realize I have a lot to be proud of.

**Outcome #3: Scholastic achievement and aspirations**

Staff encourage me to do well in school.

Program activities have helped me want to learn more about new things.

Program activities have helped me want to try harder in school.

**Outcome #4: Encourage "Y" core values**

Staff create opportunities for me to help others.

Staff expect me to take responsibility for planning and leading activities.

Staff expect me to respect others' feelings and property.

Staff expect me to help out.

Activities have helped me stand up for what I believe even when it's unpopular to do so.

Activities have helped me to be more caring towards others.

Activities have helped me to be more honest, even when it's not easy.

**Outcome #5: Improved or emerging skills**

Activities have helped me make better decisions.

Activities have helped me get along well with others.

Activities have helped me to make new friends.

Activities have helped me learn how to be a leader.

Activities have helped me learn I can do things I didn't think I could do.

Overall, how would rate these activities?

Would you recommend these activities to a friend?

The same Y gives a survey to parents whose children participate in Y camps:

The camp program is *(circle all that apply)*: fun, challenging, interesting

Compared to other places where my child spends time (like school or in my neighborhood), when s/he is at YMCA camp, s/he feels *(circle one)*: safer, just as safe, less safe

[Response options for the following questions are strongly agree, agree, disagree, strongly disagree.]

**The adults who work with camp . . .**

1. really care about my child.
2. make my child feel like s/he belongs.
3. listen to what my child has to say.
4. challenge my child to do his/her best.
5. expect my child to follow the rules.
6. expect my child to respect others' feelings and property.
7. are approachable and my child likes them.
8. try to understand my child.

**Being involved in camp . . .**

9. has made my child eager to learn about new things.

10. has taught my child rules about what's okay and what isn't.

11. my child has felt good about his/her accomplishments.

12. my child's confidence has grown.

13. my child has felt safe.

**Camp has helped my child . . .**

14. make better decisions.

15. get a better sense of what s/he can do.

16. learn s/he can do things s/he didn't think s/he could do.

17. get along with campers.

18. make and keep friends.

19. feel successful in the activities s/he has been a part of.

**At camp, my child has learned . . .**

20. about nature and how to keep the earth clean.

21. s/he has a lot to be proud of.

22. about other cultures and how to get along.

23. to care more for others.

24. how to work with others to reach goals.

25. s/he has to keep up with his/her own belongings.

Here is introductory information, as well as the main questions, from a more extensive survey Search Institute developed for use in YMCAs:

The YMCA Youth Survey is intended to ask about your participation in YMCA activities and to get important information about what you think and feel about these activities. The survey will help the YMCA to make its programs better. It will take about 10–20 minutes to complete.

Your answers on this questionnaire will be kept strictly confidential. Do not put your name on this form. The YMCA will receive a report that combines all answers together. No one will be able to connect your answers with your name.

This is not a test that has right and wrong answers. You are just being asked to tell about yourself and your experiences. Please be honest. We are doing this to help improve activities at your YMCA. Your answers will make a difference!

In some of the questions, we will ask you about your experience at the YMCA in general. In other questions, we will ask you about your experience in a specific program. If you are not sure what program you are in, please ask an adult.

**About You**

1. How old are you?
2. Are you male or female?
3. Which best describes you? Please mark only one.
   - ➤ American Indian
   - ➤ Asian or Pacific Islander
   - ➤ Black or African American
   - ➤ Hispanic, Latino, or Latina
   - ➤ White or Caucasian
   - ➤ Multiracial
4. Which one of the following best describes your family?
   - ➤ I live with two parents.
   - ➤ I live in a one-parent family with my mother.
   - ➤ I live in a one-parent family with my father.
   - ➤ Sometimes I live with my mother and sometimes with my father.
   - ➤ I live with another guardian, relative, or person(s) other than my parents.
   - ➤ I don't know.
5. Do you get a free or reduced price lunch at school?
6. Do you or your family have a membership at the YMCA?
   - ➤ My family has a membership.
   - ➤ I'm the only one in my family with a membership.
   - ➤ No one in my family is a member.
   - ➤ I don't know.

**What You Did Today**

7. Which program or activity are you here for today?
8. How often do you come to this program or activity?
9. Please answer the following for the program or activity you are in today. How much do you agree or disagree with each of the following [strongly agree, agree, disagree, strongly disagree]?

A. The program has been fun.

B. The program has been interesting.

C. The program has been challenging.

10. How long have you been involved in any YMCA programs or activities?

11. During the last six months, about how many hours a week did you spend at the YMCA or in any YMCA activities?

12. Have you been involved in any of these types of YMCA programs or activities in the last year? (Ask an adult if you are unsure.)

A. Youth sports and recreation (such as basketball)

B. Youth leadership and service

C. Camp program

D. Mentoring program

E. Drop-in or teen center

F. Other after-school programs

G. Youth employment or job readiness activities

H. Special event (such as holiday parties or tournaments)

I. Other activities

13. Overall, how good a job have YMCA programs and activities done in helping you learn more about yourself and your strengths?

➤ Excellent

➤ Good

➤ Fair

➤ Poor

14. How much are your parents or guardians involved in your YMCA activities or programs?

➤ Not at all involved

➤ A little involved

➤ Involved

➤ Very involved

**About How YMCA Activities Help**

We want to know if YMCA activities helped you learn or feel differently about what you do.

How much do you agree or disagree with the following [strongly agree, agree, disagree, strongly disagree]?

YMCA activities have helped me . . .

1. make better decisions.
2. get along with others.
3. make and keep friends.
4. do what is right even when other kids want to do something else.
5. deal with people who are being mean or starting fights.
6. learn how to be a leader.
7. be a better team player.
8. be better at sports.
9. stay away from drugs.
10. stay out of trouble.
11. feel good about myself.
12. have a lot to be proud of.
13. get a better sense of what I can do.
14. learn that what I do makes a difference.
15. learn I can do things I didn't think I could do.
16. feel successful in the activities I have been a part of.

How much do you agree or disagree with each of the following [strongly agree, agree, disagree, strongly disagree]?

17. People at the YMCA try to teach me the difference between right and wrong.
18. At YMCA activities, I've learned it's important to help other people.
19. Being in YMCA activities makes me want to learn more about new things.
20. People in Y activities expect me to respect others' feelings and property.
21. Participation in Y activities has made me want to try harder in school.
22. People at the Y expect me to help out in some way by setting up, cleaning up, or being in charge of things.
23. People at the YMCA encourage me to do well in school.

Since you have been coming to the YMCA, have the following become more or less important to you [much more, more, less, much less]?
24. Caring about other people.

25. Thinking that everyone has something to contribute.
26. Treating all people fairly.
27. Standing up for what I believe, even when it's unpopular to do so.
28. Telling the truth, even when it's not easy.
29. Being responsible for what I do.
30. Understanding and caring about other people's feelings.

**About People**

We would like to ask you about adults at the YMCA or who are in YMCA activities. These include YMCA staff and program leaders as well as other adults you have contact with through YMCA programs.

How much do you agree or disagree with each of the following [strongly agree, agree, disagree, strongly disagree]?

1. YMCA staff and program leaders really care about me.
2. Staff and program leaders make me feel important.
3. I could go to an adult at the YMCA for advice if I had a serious problem.
4. I really like the people who run YMCA activities.
5. In YMCA activities, I am given a chance to help others.
6. YMCA staff and program leaders understand me.
7. Staff and program leaders listen to what I have to say.
8. I get to help plan, choose, or lead activities.
9. YMCA staff and program leaders challenge me to do my best.
10. I feel safe when I am in YMCA activities.
11. Other YMCA kids care about me.
12. Staff make me feel like I can make a difference.
13. Other adults who hang out here care about me.
14. People make me feel like I belong.
15. In YMCA activities, I do things to help out.
16. In YMCA activities, adults expect the best from me.
17. Compared to other places I spend time (like school or in my neighborhood), when I am in YMCA programs or activities, I feel . . .
    ➤ safer
    ➤ just as safe
    ➤ less safe

**About YMCA Activities**

Now we want to ask you more questions about YMCA programs and activities.

How much do you agree or disagree with each of the following [strongly agree, agree, disagree, strongly disagree]?

18. I am expected to try hard and do my best.
19. There are clear rules about what we can and cannot do.
20. If I break one of the rules, I usually hear about it.
21. There are clear rules about not smoking or drinking alcohol.

Among your friends from YMCA activities, how many would you say . . . [Response options are none, a few, some, most, almost all.]

22. do well in school?
23. drink alcohol once a week or more?
24. care about others?
25. get into trouble at school?

**About Other Things You Do**

We are interested in what else you do and how you spend your time.

During a week, about how many hours do you spend [1, 2, 3, 4–5, more than 5 hours, none] . . .

1. doing community service or volunteer work (like helping older people, cleaning up parks, tutoring younger children)?
2. playing on or helping with sports teams at school or in the community?
3. in clubs or organizations (other than sports) at school?
4. going to programs, groups, or services at a church, synagogue, mosque, or other religious or spiritual place?
5. doing homework outside school?
6. in YMCA activities or programs?
7. in other clubs or activities outside school (like Scouts, 4-H, Camp Fire)?
8. in community service or volunteer work at the YMCA?

In the last 12 months, how many times, if any, have you [once, twice, a few times, many times, never] . . .

9. had alcohol to drink?

10. smoked cigarettes?

11. used drugs such as marijuana or cocaine?

12. taken part in a fight where a group of your friends fought another group?

13. threatened to physically hurt someone?

14. skipped school?

15. been suspended or dropped out of school?

*How do you monitor what your organization is actually doing?*

*How do you assess how well it's doing it?*

*Are you getting systematic feedback from staff?*

*From youth?*

*From parents?*

*From your community?*

*Are you getting both qualitative and quantitative data?*

*How do you make your assessments useful and non-threatening?*

### A General Rule and a Word of Caution

I've included these examples to give you an opportunity to use what works for you. But let me give you one general rule and one common caution about assessment. The rule: Get information from as many different, appropriate sources as you can in as many different, appropriate ways as you can. That means at least staff, administrators, parents, and especially young people. That means at least interviews, questionnaires, observation, and focus groups.

And the common caution (it's common because it's seldom heeded): Be sure that your tools are constructed to give you the information you want—no more, no less. The longer people have to spend wading through questions, the less likely they'll think about them carefully—common sense, right?—and the less reliable your data will be. And getting reams of information won't benefit anyone if you don't know how to analyze the data, don't know how to interpret what you do analyze, and don't know how to use what you do interpret. So be sure to tread carefully. Monitoring is critical, but, like any strategy, it should do what it's intended to do.

*The most effective programs relate to teenagers according to where the young people are "at," instead of where the professional staff think they ought to be.*

—JOY DRYFOOS, *Safe Passage: Making It through Adolescence in a Risky Society* (1998)

# 4

# Walking Programs and Activities

The question now is this: What kinds of programs and activities provide young people with opportunities to build assets? It would be far easier if programs came with a stamp of approval: "This program has been shown to be an effective tool in promoting developmental assets in young people." But such is not the case—and because so much rides on the individual, unique relationships established between adult and young person, it's likely never to be the case. The program itself is only part of the story; the proof of this pudding is often in the implementation and in the staffing. Nonetheless, we do have some information about which strategies in general are more likely to produce the assets we're interested in. Karen VanderVen is a professor in the University of Pittsburgh's Department of Psychology in Education; she has written extensively on how to meaningfully involve young people in activities—with the focus on the young person. Here are some of her suggested techniques:

**Developing/sustaining an "activity culture,"** showing continuous focus on, and immersion in, activities;

**Avoiding tying activities to "good behavior" or "earning activities";** this ultimately increases poor behavior and teaches young people not to care about or show interest in activities;

**Orderly, inviting environment** with interest areas, a sufficient number of materials attractively arranged;

**Showing adult enthusiasm,** modeling energy, investment, interest in the activity;

**Serving as a "co-ego,"** providing immediate, ongoing support and refocusing on activity if necessary, breaking task down into doable chunks;

**Avoiding power struggles,** without abandoning control—not pressuring a resistant child . . . allowing [a child] to save face, continuing . . . despite laggards;

**Building on symptom / interest patterns,** using both psychological characteristics and expressed interests as a bridge to activities;

**Positive expectations,** approaching young people . . . with an attitude of "Of course you'll join in" and "You can do it!"

**Novelty effect,** providing something new, which inevitably generates interest and attention;

**Showing ongoing interest,** asking young people how their activities are coming along;

**Judicious use of praise,** avoiding meaningless or constant praise; and

**Encouraging performance standards,** nudging young people towards higher level and recognizing each new level; encouraging the development of internal standards.

These are excellent guidelines. How do you put them all together into an activity that truly builds assets? I can tell you that there are thousands of such activities taking place every day across this country. The activities may focus on only one asset or on many. They may involve one young person at a time or a group of young people. Some of the facilitators of the activities are intentionally building assets, while others are not. Some are explicitly discussing the asset framework with young people, while others are not.

In El Paso, young people have facilitated reading circles, music classes, community discussions, recycling programs, and a multitude of panels and presentations. And the regional youth council put on Jamfest 2001, a music festival. Thirty young people planned it, created ads for it, videotaped a documentary about it—and almost weren't allowed to put it on. The manager of the stadium that the youth had contracted for the event took a look at the attendance several hours before the event, saw about 200 people, and went out for lunch. When he came back an hour later, the number had burgeoned to more than 4,000. Fearing that fighting or vandalism was inevitable, the manager panicked and called the police. A group of youth and adults immediately entered into negotiations with the manager; they assured him that the event was under control because of the number of youth volunteers, adult volunteers, and security present. The manager relented and eventually asked the police to stick around during the event instead of stopping it. The show, as they say, went on. An asset-building activity? Of course. Intentional? Only part of it. But when you're thinking along the lines of youth as resources and not as problems, then good things happen.

Let me present to you one activity that I think is as asset-rich as any I've seen. It's simple, it's based on relationships, and, what's more, it makes use of previously existing relationships. It comes from the Paso del Norte Foundation, and I want to present it, for the most part, as it appears in the Executive Project Summary from the Action for Youth 2001 Project Proposal, so that you understand the full rationale for the activity:

> There is a trend taking place in this country. One in ten grandparents have been the primary support of a grandchild at some time in their lives. Currently, six percent of children live in a grandparent-headed household. Whatever the reason and situation, these grandparents face a range of difficulties, including legal and policy challenges. Many organizations that provide services for both generations are not prepared to deal with the special needs and situations presented. Legal options are limited and emotionally draining and expensive. Few attorneys are familiar with the relevant laws. In most states, statutes are not responsive to the evolving needs of grandparents who wish to have more permanent rights for guardianship of their grandchildren.
>
> Grandchildren are often forced to live with grandparents because of tragedy, abandonment, poor family economics, and substance abuse,

among others. Grandparents, on the other hand, often experience feelings of being alone and unsupported, ashamed, guilty, frightened, and confused when their grandchildren live with them.

. . . [We intend] to assist grandparents to increase the involvement of their grandchildren in the care process, focusing on the following assets:

➤ **Family support:** finding ways to enhance the grandparent/ grandchild relationship;

➤ **Positive family communication:** increasing grandchildren's willingness to seek advice and counsel from grandparents;

➤ **Family boundaries:** helping grandchildren learn that rules are necessary to monitor [their] whereabouts;

➤ **Caring:** enhancing the grandchildren's appreciation for helping other grandchildren cope with new relationships with grandparents;

➤ **Planning and decision making:** helping grandchildren understand the importance of looking ahead and making decisions in their and their grandparents' own best interest;

➤ **Peaceful conflict resolution:** helping grandchildren deal positively with conflict in the new grandchild/grandparent relationship;

➤ **Self-esteem:** helping grandchildren develop new ways to view their positive accomplishments to enhance self-image; and

➤ **Sense of purpose:** helping grandchildren develop new life goals and objectives that fit with their strengths and capabilities.

. . . [The Committee plans] to . . . support regular meetings of grandparents and grandchildren in the 12–18 years group. More specifically, we will meet regularly with the grandparents the first Monday morning and second Tuesday evening each month to debate and discuss how the assets listed above could best be incorporated in grandparent/grandchild discussions to increase their usefulness and acceptance in the household. Then the participating grandchildren will meet with our staff on the third Monday each month after school to discuss the assets and how best, from their own point of view, to incorporate them into the family relationship. . . .

The Committee [also plans] to support three workshops to provide the grandchildren an expanded forum for discussion of asset-based

topics and to learn from each other. Grandparents would be in attendance as observers. The grandchildren would be directly involved in
the planning for these workshops, setting the agenda and presenting
the topics themselves. . . .

We propose to purchase video equipment . . . to enable us to record
these workshops on videotape. Appropriate participating youth with
audio-visual skills will be recruited to do the actual videotaping of the
workshops. These resulting videos would be made available to other
organizations or agencies wishing to learn about youth's own views
and approach to enhancing grandchildren/grandparents communication to better reach objectives as incorporated in the assets listed
above.

There are some great things about this activity. As I mentioned, it builds
on existing relationships. But it has some very interesting other features:
It meets a social need. It serves a wide range of young people (and
adults). It gives the participants both the opportunity and the responsibility for choosing and delivering content. It's self-perpetuating. It contains a component—the videos—that, in a sense, enables it to reproduce.
And it can be facilitated by a variety of organizations that serve youth—
most likely yours.

All these programs and activities depend on building partnerships
with young people in one form or another, so that's how I've labeled
them. Following the next section, I'll focus on two other types of partnerships—one with organizations, and the other with families.

## Partnerships with Young People

*"The 'magic' happens when we capture the passion of youth and give it focus
and direction to create change. The change first happens in the youth themselves.
Then they become able to share their knowledge and skills with someone else.
Finally, the 'magic' spreads to the chapter, the school, and the community."*

—PAMELA VOSS-PAGE, executive director,
Student Leadership Services, Inc., Waterford, Michigan

Let's look at some more programs and activities. I've arranged them by
the themes of service, leadership, and personal development, but I could

have organized them in any of several other ways. Because of their rich-ness and adaptability, programs and activities such as these don't always fall neatly into categories, but I think you'll be able to appreciate the gist of each of them.

### Service

Don't ever let anyone tell you that youth aren't thinking about assets. Recently, Keith Pattinson, the regional director of the Boys and Girls Clubs of British Columbia, spoke to 330 6th- and 7th-grade students at an asset-building workshop and, after describing the developmental assets framework, asked them to complete the following sentence: "When I leave here today, here's what I'll try to do to help kids my age and younger . . ." After five minutes, he asked if they were ready, but he got the impression that they needed more time. Five minutes later, he got the same impression. Finally, after another five minutes, he stopped the exer-cise, thinking that it had been too difficult. No doubt he was more sur-prised than the participants when the final count was tallied, several days later—2,500 different ideas for building assets. Some examples:

> ➤ "I'll go to school and help some people who don't understand questions."
> ➤ "I'll tie little kids' shoelaces."
> ➤ "I'll give them a putup instead of a putdown."
> ➤ "I'll stick up for someone younger."
> ➤ "I'll say hi when I pass by."

What *have* young people accomplished? Read the following profile of an enterprise called Teen Closet. This is taken from the spring/summer 2001 issue of the *MakingTime* newsletter, edited by Robin Haaseth for the It's About Time for Kids group in Bellevue, Washington.

### A RESOURCE TAILORED FOR TEENS

Their shopping bags are full. Two teen boys have just selected a jacket and a few outfits. The boys' father stops to shake hands with RJ Sam-mons, Ground Zero Teen Center Director. The father says a simple and very sincere, "Thank you. Thank you very much." Sammons responds, "Thank you for coming." This isn't a scene from a clothing store at Bellevue Square. The family is visiting Teen Closet, a unique clothing bank in Bellevue, designed just for teens.

On the second Thursday of each month, the Ground Zero Teen Center's basement is transformed into a mini-boutique, offering a wide variety of new and "very gently used" clothing. There are several crowded racks loaded with coats, sweaters, shorts, shirts, and pants. Colorful outfits hang as wall displays.

All of the clothing at Teen Closet is free. "Most of the donations come from moms who are cleaning out closets and they call to see if we can use these clothes. We also had a great donation from Polo Jean Company of new clothes valued at about $17,000. But these are almost gone now and we could use a lot more," said Sammons.

The idea for Teen Closet began with a phone call from Karen Butler of ASSISTEENS, an auxiliary of the Assistance League of the Eastside, to Ellen Curtis, interim Youth Link Program Coordinator. ASSISTEENS had just collected teen clothing and she called Curtis to see if she knew of young people who could use it. "I presented the information to the Bellevue Youth Council and the whole idea (to start a clothing bank) snowballed from there," Curtis said.

Teen Closet is a partnership of Bellevue Youth Link, ASSISTEENS, and the Bellevue Boys and Girls Club, who operates the teen center located in downtown Bellevue. The program is run by staff and volunteers and needs ongoing help to keep it running. Volunteers are important, says Sammons. He organizes a weekly volunteer party where volunteers also can help those that need help "digging through and finding things—the right size, or what looks good," he says.

It's a lot of work, but Sammons is pleased with the project. "When you see a family and teens come in and they're so thankful, you really see you're serving a need."

Another example, this one from Tommy Tinajero of Paso del Norte about "Landscape Projects":

This project will promote developmental assets through community landscape projects that will take place in early summer 2001, early fall 2001, and spring 2002. Youth, parent, and adult volunteers will be recruited from the community to install and renovate landscapes in at least four communities served by the partnership. . . .

Adult volunteers with various skill levels will be recruited for the project, and they will be encouraged to mentor the youth. Since land-

scape projects often immerse participants in a nonthreatening environment, there will be increased opportunities for mentoring. . . .

During these projects, a review of one or more developmental
assets will be conducted. We specifically hope to (1) engage the youth
to care for their environment and provide service to others, (2) promote mentoring between the adults and youth, (3) engage the community's support and involvement in identifying landscapes or other areas
that deserve the community's attention, and (4) encourage the youth
and adults to plan and implement landscape construction or installa-
tion projects. The landscape projects selected will meet or surpass the
skill level of the participants. This will provide the youth with opportunities to learn a skill. Also, the youth will be involved in training
community members and other youth to maintain landscapes. . . .

This project will serve as an avenue for youth and adults in under-
served communities to enhance their outdoor living space and learn
relevant life skills. By engaging in real-world projects, the youth will
learn problem-solving skills in a real environment. The intergenerational landscaping project will work collaboratively with the physical
and creative partnerships. This project will facilitate community
service components of those partnerships.

David Kelly-Hedrick, director of the Institute for Youth Service and
Leadership, an offshoot of the YMCA of Greater Seattle, describes an
"environmental justice symposium" that not only exemplifies service, it
virtually bursts with asset building. Twelve teams, each comprising 12
teenagers, went into the community to perform service projects or interview people about significant issues. On each team a teenage photog-
rapher documented the team's activities. At the conclusion of their foray
into the community, the teams each created a 3'-x-3' wood panel with a
collage of relevant images, words, and documents. The panels were then
put together, and a mural was created for the opposite side. The result
was similar to a room divider, and it has been exhibited at various gal-
leries in the Northwest. Service, creativity, self-esteem—you can go
down the list of assets and see how an activity like this can accomplish
so many things.

### Leadership

What have young people accomplished? At the Christie School, the residents have input into programs that affect them and their peers. One boy

separated from his sister lobbied for siblings staying together when assigned to residential treatment centers. And when residents "move on," the others traditionally throw them going-away parties.

Alternatives, Inc., operates out of Hampton, Virginia; it forms partnerships with schools, community groups, and city offices to create environments that value young people as community resources. The organization does this with a variety of programs, training, and curricula aimed at young people from ages 8 to 18. Here are a few of the projects mentioned in Alternatives, Inc.'s 1999–2000 annual report:

In the Hampton City Schools, young people worked side by side with principals and administrators on school improvement committees facilitated by Alternatives. The primary goal for the year was to identify ways to create more caring and respectful school environments. The culmination of their efforts was the highly successful CARE (Creating A Respectful Environment) School Improvement Conference. Teams of students, parents, and school staff from each middle and high school in Hampton participated in lively strategy sessions that produced plans for creating caring environments in their particular school. Plans for the 2000/2001 school year include implementation of peer mentoring programs and projects to increase support for students in transition. In addition, both students and teachers can take part in workshops, trainings and promotions designed to cultivate a caring learning environment.

In the community, YouthWorks has become one of the most exciting and promising community-based programs developed by Alternatives. Begun this past year, the employment readiness curriculum for young people 15 to 21 years of age is a real win-win for youth and employers. Young people who sign up for the 7 week courses learn the type of attitudes and behaviors needed to get and be successful in a job. Employers, in turn, are assured that they will be getting a more motivated and hardworking employee. . . .

In our neighborhood groups, young people continued their work with adults on projects large and small. Together they developed long-range plans, after-school recreational and academic activities, cleanups, career and health fairs, and other community-building events. The crime reduction projects in the Newtown and Tyler-Seldondale neighborhoods are beginning to show incredible reductions in juvenile crime statistics.

And now we come to Cary, North Carolina. All sorts of asset building through youth leadership are happening in this town and nearby communities. For one thing, Cary's youth group—called C.A.R.Y., for Creating Assets Reaching Youth—has its own Web site, www.cary-youth.org, that is managed by Jeremy Guzman, 17, who helped design the site and has been working on it for three years. The Web site is professional and informative. Here are some excerpts:

### Mission Statement

Developmental assets are the essential building blocks that young people need for successful growth and development. To that end, C.A.R.Y. is a place where we all grow together by uniting asset-building capabilities of our community to support the development of healthy, caring, responsible youth.

### Vision Statement

Uniting the Cary community to nurture asset development in youth.

### CARY Goals for 2001 [partial list]

➤ Maintain Speakers Bureau
➤ Increase corporate support and participation in Cary Chamber of Commerce
➤ Continue leadership and sponsorship for Youth Page
➤ Continue leadership of SK8-CARY
➤ Conduct/Facilitate two youth forums and five community forums
➤ Youth Hall of Fame recognition at 2002 Youth Matter to Cary Day
➤ Continue leadership and sponsorship of Red Ribbon Poster Contest Day and Youth Matter to Cary Day
➤ Focus more on building active and supportive relationships between youth and others in the community

That's not all that's going on in Cary. Hannah Litzenburger, 14, is the Youth Page editor for the *Cary News*, which typically reaches 20,000 people. The youth page highlights projects that young people in the community have done as well as issues that affect them. Here are some highlights from the Thursday, September 27, 2001, issue:

### Cameras Cameras Everywhere!

A discussion of the controversy surrounding the number of security cameras, "bike cops," and police officers at Cary High School, with quotes from the vice principal and candidates for the town council.

### There is Something to Do!

The article discusses the rationale for extracurricular activities and suggestions of local Web sites, activities, and clubs.

### What is council going to do for youth?

Each of 13 candidates for the At-Large, District A, and District C seats was asked, "If elected, what are you going to do to support the youth of Cary?" The article presents their responses along with their color photograph.

### Is this the best Cary has to offer?

## SKATE PARK GROUNDBREAKING CAPS OFF
## A YEAR OF HARD WORK AND DEDICATION

No, not any more! With the new **SK8–CARY** skate park under construction, soon youth can come and board, blade, and bike all they want at the best skate park in North Carolina. They won't have to skate on the streets and sidewalks and get into trouble. Great news for all you parents out there. It's going to be a skate park where safety comes first. The new skate park will be built at Godbold Park on Northwest Maynard Road (to see the designs, go to www.cary-youth.org).

It all started about eighteen months ago when Matt Espy and Max Killian went knocking on Mayor Lang's door. They told him that they needed a place to skateboard because the police were running them off everywhere they were boarding. Mayor Lang told them that Mrs. Liza Weidle would be a good person to help with this situation because she is involved a lot with the youth in the community. So after many long hours and early rising for fundraising and planning, the skate park should be finished by the beginning of February.

The skate park construction will start in about two weeks. The contractor for building the skate park states that it will take one hundred and twenty calendar days. The ramps will be made of wood covered with Skate Light Pro. There will be three half pipes (five to six feet high) and a street course. From the looks of the design it seems to be a challenging skate park. So all you skateboarders out there, get ready for serious action. The facility will have a full staff, a concession stand, picnic tables, and a girl's and a boy's bathroom. The viewing area (for all you moms and dads) will be about six feet high to protect you from flying skateboards. Overall, the SK8-CARY skate park is going to be extremely cool and a great addition to the community for the youth. As a fellow skateboarder, we should be very thankful and pleased with what Cary has given to its youth.

—Davis Litzenburger

CALLING ALL YOUTH who have an interest in writing, photography, and cartooning! How would you like to have your work published in the news for the entire community to experience? HAVE WE GOT A JOB FOR YOU! If you are a middle or high school student interested in helping to create a Youth Page like this one visit WWW.CARYYOUTH.ORG or contact Harold or Hannah Litzenburger. . . .

If you are working on this page, you will be building the following ASSETS. **Asset #8:** You will have a useful role in the community. **Asset #17:** You will be participating in a creative activity. **Asset #18:** You will be spending three or more hours per week in sports, clubs, or organizations at school and/or in community organizations. **Asset #23:** You will be actively engaged in learning. **Asset #29:** You will be valuing responsibility.

What have young people accomplished? There are examples all over North America. Kelly Greenwell, the youth and family coordinator in Victoria, British Columbia, says that he's been amazed at how quickly young people learn skills and take on responsibilities. Whether it's youth at the Mosaic Youth Center organizing open-microphone nights or young people at the Tillamook County Family YMCA producing a 34-minute video introducing assets and the local efforts to build them; whether it's teenagers on the High Point Asset Team planning classes on SAT preparation and computer training or middle and high school students in Brownsville, Kentucky, facilitating after-school programs for 4th- and 5th-grade students—young people continue to accomplish great things.

**Personal Development**

Young people are "personally developing" all the time. But when you apply the asset framework, you're giving them opportunities to develop their capabilities, to expand their boundaries, to relate to one another, and to understand and feel good about themselves.

Camps are a fertile location for such activities. Here's an example from Robin Haaseth, the coordinator of It's about Time for Kids in Bellevue, Washington, who works in the city's Parks and Community Services Department. She received this information from Pamela Myers, who participated in the Kids' Connection Day Camp:

> The camps selected two assets to focus on. This information was on the back of a flyer that went to every participant: Self-esteem and Creative activities.
>
> These two were very easy assets to work on every day. Each day the children were involved in art projects, singing and sometimes skits, scavenger hunts, and a variety of other creative activities. We did not limit the creative activities to just art, as each child has . . . unique creative talents. Self-esteem was emphasized in different ways. For example, at the end of the week the kids went home with a note (on fun paper) about their outstanding qualities. Other ways were having the parents invited to an activity on Friday that focused on what the children were doing.
>
> At each camp there were posters with the assets listed in an artistic manner. Other posters were made throughout the summer. Some were kids' quotes. Artwork was displayed, as well as photos of the kids with an asset written under picture, and whatever else we could think of.
>
> . . . We feel it is important to make the assets an everyday part of the program and not necessarily something that takes time out of the day. The idea is for the staff and parents to automatically implement as many assets into the day as possible.

I want to present to you more examples of small-group activities that provide opportunities for young people to build assets. I'm choosing a fairly wide range so that you can come away with an appreciation of the spectrum of possibilities for your own organization. This next example is another from Paso del Norte; it's called WyldLife:

WyldLife is an effort to promote the knowledge, attitudes, and practice of Search Institute's 40 developmental assets through weekly gath-
erings [on] Friday night . . .

At WyldLife youth and volunteers will be involved in games that
will be designed to build relationships with other adults (#3) and
teach the importance of youth as a resource (#8). Skits and role-
playing will be aimed at building integrity (#28), sense of purpose
(#32), planning and decision making (#39). . . .

The most important aspect of this project is to develop relationships between youth and adults through interaction, building self-
esteem in the youths, playing, and sharing constructive time together.

In the preceding chapter, we met Tricia Segal, the coordinator of
young adult services at the Fort Vancouver Regional Library, in Vancouver, Washington. Using survey results from Clark County, she developed programs targeting assets that teenagers reported low levels of
experiencing. Here's a description of an activity that she coordinated:

The Clark County Juvenile Detention Center [JDC] was awarded a
grant from First Book in October 2000. The grant allowed for the purchase of 12 copies of 24 titles of both fiction and nonfiction that would
be used for book discussion at the JDC. Trish Segal, the Coordinator
of Young Adult Services for the Fort Vancouver Regional Library,
facilitates the ordering, distribution, and discussion of the books.
Trish visits the JDC twice a month to hold book discussions. The first
part of the month the teens read a fiction book, and the last part of the
month they read a nonfiction book. The teens who participate in the
book discussion get special permission to keep the books in their
room and get to keep them when they are released so they can begin
to build their own personal library.

The book discussion has had a wonderful effect on the teens in
JDC. They have been taking better care of the books in the library
there, and they share their copies of books with other inmates. They
have even begun holding their own book discussions when Trish is
not there and have been recommending books to one another.

Many of the youth have reported to Trish that they do not read
"on the outs," and that they read their first book in JDC. One teen said
that the book he got from the discussion was the first book he's ever

owned. Many of the teens are very poor readers, but they've become motivated to improve their reading skills in order to participate in the discussions.

Some books discussed so far are:

*Harry Potter and the Sorcerer's Stone*, by J. K. Rowling

*Harry Potter and the Chamber of Secrets*, by J. K. Rowling

*Snowbound: The Tragic Story of the Donner Party*,
    by David Lavender

*Calvin and Hobbes*, by Bill Watterson

*You Be the Detective*, by Marvin Miller

*Within Reach: My Everest Story*, by Mark Pfetzer and
    Jack Galvin

*Scorpions*, by Walter Dean Myers

*The Golden Compass*, by Philip Pullman

*Woodsong*, by Gary Paulsen

What do I think is the most significant sentence in that description? "They have even begun holding their own book discussions when Trish is not there and have been recommending books to one another." When we teach social skills—such as resistance skills—to students, we call that the "transfer" step: What do they do after we're gone? In this case, the transfer worked marvelously. The teenagers were instilled with the love of reading; a facilitator was no longer necessary to motivate them.

That's asset building.

Here's another example from Robin Haaseth; it's an article she wrote for the fall 2000 *MakingTime* newsletter of the Bellevue, Washington, asset-building initiative:

### YOUTH EXPLORE FUTURE CAREERS

He sits in the front row at the edge of a low bench. He is grinning, his feet are tapping, and his head is nodding. Joey McDaniel, a 17-year-old junior at Sammamish High School in Bellevue, is enjoying a music video about "funk" at the Experience Music Project in Seattle. He is touring with a group of approximately 20 high school students of various cultural backgrounds who have gathered for a week of career exploration through a City of Bellevue program called Youth at Hope.

"I have no idea what career I'd like," said Dan Harvey, 15. "I like (the Youth at Hope program) because I get to see stuff I wouldn't normally see." The program allows students to explore careers and helps them to find adult mentors in potential career fields. McDaniel, who is an aspiring musician, also dreams of being a fashion designer. "When they came to my school and told me I could get hooked up with a mentor, I said, I'm on that. Music, cosmetology, fashion, it all goes together . . . it's image. I would really like to work in all of those areas," said McDaniel.

The one-week summer program includes traditional opportunities for career exploration such as speakers at Bellevue City Hall and tours of technical and community colleges. It also includes exploration of nontraditional careers. . . .

Youth at Hope is designed to help youth by bringing them together to learn about themselves and their potential. "Things like sports and music bring cultures together," said Kevin Henry, Youth at Hope program organizer. "They break down the barriers between people."

Jeanne Harvey Duncan, working with Seattle's Sound Youth, developed an after-school theater program called CAST with low-achieving, homeless students—anywhere from 12 to 25 young people. Among CAST's features:

> Students were tutored after school;
> Once a week they'd be transported to Seaview Methodist Church, where they'd spend two to three hours helping to produce a play—everything from *Mulan* to *A Midsummer's Night Dream*—and share a meal; and
> They would perform the play in front of groups of 25–500 people.

And, based on reports from the students' parents, teachers, and the students themselves, what did they learn from the experience?

> They learned about drama by writing about various characters in the play and discussing what the characters would look and act like;
> They learned about sound, lighting, and set design;
> They learned about sharing, helping each other, and even such mundane activities as cleaning up after a meal;
> They improved their literacy skills by reading scripts and memorizing lines;

> ➤ They built relationships with the director and other adults;

> ➤ They raised their awareness of themselves and others; and

> ➤ They increased their confidence and self-esteem.

Duncan, an ordained minister, uses the asset framework with her congregation. She also used a strength-based approach when forging relationships with the CAST students. Duncan remembers a six-year-old Cambodian refugee learning English and living in a large, extended family. She desperately wanted to be in the play they were producing, but she was too shy and her English too poor to act. Nonetheless, the people involved in the play developed a nonspeaking part for her. She performed, and both she and her parents were thrilled. Asset building in action.

What seems to be the ultimate in an asset-building activity was developed by Susan Allen, director of the Wisconsin Positive Youth Development Initiative, in Westfield, Wisconsin. Allen started an organization called Teen Power, which is based on the asset framework. Much of what the 36 teenagers involved in Teen Power do is what Allen calls community improvement (she believes that community "service" is perceived as punitive). The young people identify conditions in their community that are good and other conditions that aren't so good; then they figure out what they can do to make a difference. They plan all their projects and events—determining where to get financial support, what tasks to accomplish by whom and by when, and what success will inevitably look like. Then they carry out what they planned. The secret to the effectiveness of activities like these? The young people are in charge.

But one of Allen's activities has nothing to do with community improvement and everything to do with individual improvement. It's called "Follow Your Dream," and it works like this: Using money from state grants—such as Law Enforcement Partnership Grants from the Division of Children and Family Services—Allen says to each teenager, "You can spend up to $100 exploring something you want to do when you grow up."

One 13-year-old girl wants to become a professional ice skater. She'd never taken a lesson before, but now she's "following her dream" at the Madison Ice Skating Academy. Another girl wants to work for the state (there can't be too many childhood fantasies of that nature), so Allen's group toured departments in the State of Wisconsin. Someone else wants to work in the Mennonite community because her baby-sitter was a Mennonite and she remembers her as peaceful; they spent a day in a nearby Mennonite community. Someone wants to become an architect; someone else wants to create video games. In every case, Allen gave the teenagers opportunities they never thought they'd have.

And then there's the boy who wants to become a sniper. This situation could be titled "When Assets Collide." Allen was in a quandary. Sniping is not exactly on the Top Ten list of careers recommended by high school guidance counselors. On the other hand, she wanted to acknowledge the boy's goals. It wasn't that he was bloodthirsty; he enjoyed marksmanship, and he wanted to serve his country. The FBI and even local police units have sharpshooters. It was, reflected Allen after much thought, a legitimate request. And so the group visited a Marine contingent in Chicago.

Who learns the lesson here? Allen says of her teenagers, "They taught me so much about asset building in action."

### Infusing Assets into Current Activities

Aside from adopting new programs like the ones I've been describing, however, what can you do with the activities you're already facilitating? When Judy Bunnell was director of the Seattle-based assets initiative, It's About Time for Kids, she used a "web of support" to help people understand how to build more assets into their current programming (see Figure 4.1). She'd have them start with a drawing of a spider web, a series of more or less concentric ovals, with radii extending from the perimeter of the central oval and forming what looked like slices of pie. Then she'd give them the following instructions:

1. In the middle of the web, write the name of the program you want to focus on (not the name of your organization).

2. Also in the middle of the web, write the name of a common activity within that program you want to focus on.

3. Yet again in the middle of the web, write the first name of a typical client/participant.

4. From the list of assets, pick several assets that you have a significant opportunity to influence during the activity you picked. Write the name of each asset in the first segment of each pie-shaped piece of the web.

5. One asset at a time, identify *additional* ways (beyond what

## Figure 4.1
## Web of Support

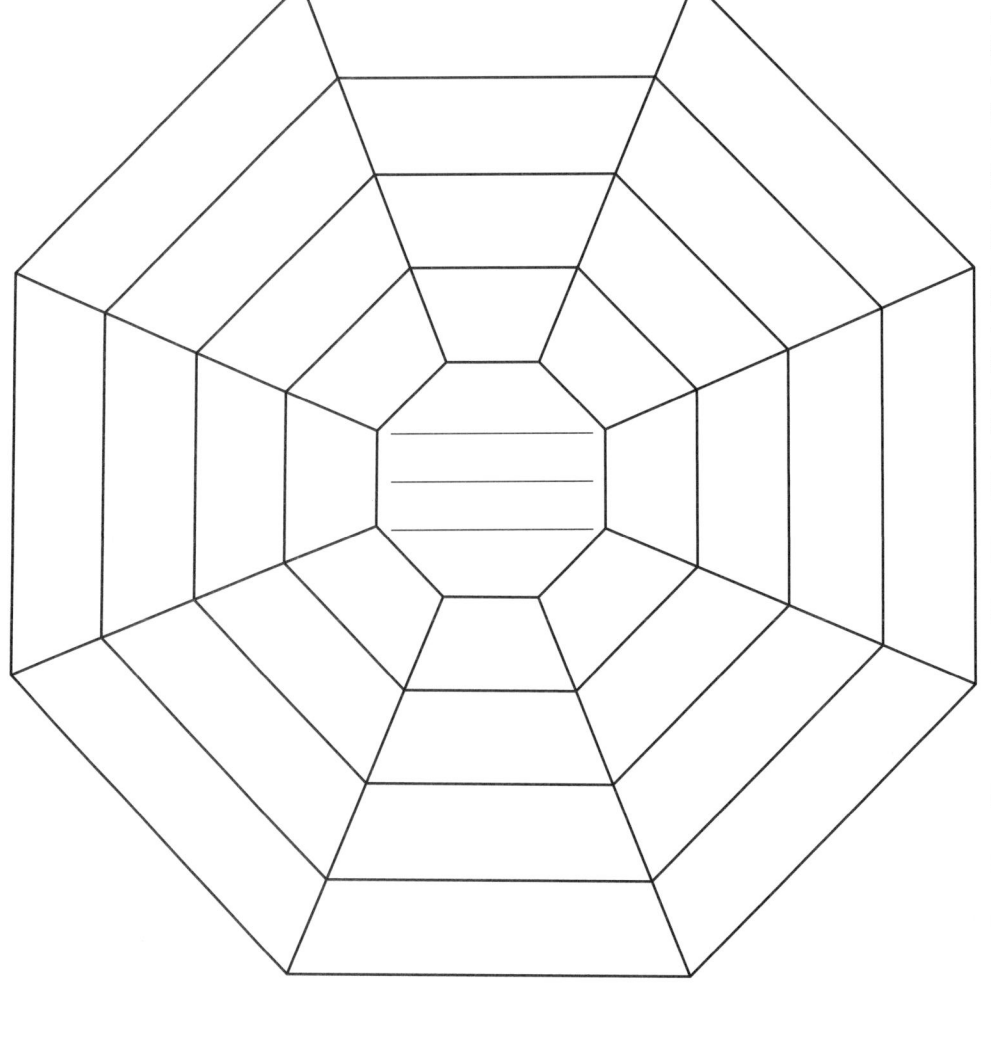

you're already doing) that you could strengthen that asset. You can think of several levels at which you might make changes:

> ➤ front-line practices and interactions with participants
> ➤ program design
> ➤ changes within your organizations, e.g., policies, environment, or staff hiring or training
> ➤ new people, resources, or connections from the community

6. Repeat this process for the other assets you identified on your web.

7. Mark three of your ideas with an asterisk to note those that you'll make it a priority to implement.

You can facilitate similar exercises with new activities and projects. In Westfield, Wisconsin, Susan Allen uses a form that includes the following information to gauge the potential impact of a project:

> ➤ Existing condition:
> ➤ Desired condition:
> ➤ Name of project:
> ➤ Description of project:
> ➤ Who (besides ourselves) will benefit from this project?
> ➤ Who needs to approve this project?
> ➤ What funds are needed? Who will get them? By when?
> ➤ How will we know if this project is successful? What will success look, sound, and feel like?

*Have the young people in your organization had opportunities to serve others in their community?*

*Have you proposed projects for them that will give them tools for their future?*

*Have you provided them with resources to help them succeed?*

*Have they had a significant role in determining what these activities will be?*

You can see that one need add only a few questions about which assets will be promoted and how they'll be promoted in order to come up with a nice, quick profile of a planned project. The Eau Claire, Wisconsin, Asset Team uses something similar called "The DO Piece to Asset Development." Each committee on their team is asked to create an action that includes the following:

> ➤ Mission (What one big asset-building goal/project you as a group are committed to accomplishing):
> ➤ Action Plan (Identify what steps will be taken, when they'll be done, and who's responsible):
> ➤ Committee Members (name, school/agency/group, address, phone, E-mail address):

What I hope I've illustrated in this section is that all these activities can be *adapted* to fit your circumstances. Moreover, the activities you've been facilitating in your organization can be *adapted* to fit the asset framework. It's not the intricate components of the activity that are important; it's how the activity is facilitated. Who's running the show? Who's participating in the show? Who can change the show? Young people have to be involved in activities and in "meta-activities" as well; they need to feel that they have something to contribute and that adults will value that contribution.

There are two gifts inside this adult-youth partnership package. The first gift is the outcome: I've described a few outcomes here, but you can imagine that thousands more exist in every town and city in the country. And the second gift is the partnership itself. Both the adult and the young person benefit from the experience—learning things about themselves and each other, working toward a common goal, doing something different, acquiring new skills. And, to return to a metaphor I used earlier when talking about monitoring, the seeds are sown for partnerships in the future.

*Which programs and activities in your organization promote assets?*

*Which programs and activities in your organization can you change to promote assets?*

*Which programs and activities might you add to promote assets?*

## Partnerships with Organizations

*"Young people immediately respond to the notion that they do indeed have value and potential. . . . Community residents are changing their perceptions about the youth in their community from 'just a bunch of troublemakers' to the valuable assets and resources that they really are."*

—SAN LUIS OBISPO COUNTY ASSET DEVELOPMENT NETWORK

2001 Jostens Our Town Award and Grant Application

Richard Enfield is the 4-H youth development advisor for the University of California's Cooperative Extension in San Luis Obispo. He says that "people can understand assets more easily than they can resiliency," and he's been making sure that people all over San Luis Obispo County— about a quarter of a million people halfway between Los Angeles and San Francisco—know about the asset framework and begin building assets intentionally with and for the young people they serve. He's worked with school principals, with parents, with neighborhoods (he's organized neighborhood block parties based on asset building), and with the

County Department of Social Services, which has adopted an asset-based approach to the extent that all its contracts have asset language in them. And of course he's worked with young people—"Teen Leaders" in high school and "Junior Leaders" in junior high school.

A community collaborative called the Asset Development Network guides asset building for the county using a four-pronged strategy: (1) educating people throughout the county about assets, (2) instituting changes in policies and social norms to be consistent with the asset framework, (3) promoting programming that builds assets with young people, and (4) developing good working relationships with seven youth task forces. The effort is coordinated by a steering committee of four organizations: the 4-H Youth Development Program, the County Department of Social Services, the County Office of Education, and the YMCA. But take a look at some of the other agencies and organizations involved in asset development in San Luis Obispo County:

➤ Action for Healthy Communities
➤ Children's Services Network
➤ Community Youth Task Forces
➤ Department of Health
➤ District Attorney's Office
➤ Drug and Alcohol Services (part of the County Health Agency)
➤ Economic Opportunity Commission
➤ Faith-based organizations
➤ Friday Night Live (partnership with County Drug and Alcohol Services)
➤ Local libraries
➤ Local municipalities and organizations (including the San Luis Obispo Police Department)
➤ Prevention Alliance
➤ Probation Department
➤ Safe Schools Integrated Prevention Project
➤ Schools
➤ Service clubs and organizations
➤ Sheriff's Department
➤ United Way of San Luis Obispo County

I present this list not to give San Luis Obispo County a chance to show off but to impress upon you the need to bring together as many sectors of your community as you can to build assets. Any one of the agencies and organizations I've listed above, including the four organizations comprising the steering committee, could have spearheaded this effort. Why is bringing sectors together important?

Let's say that you're the leader of a Girl Scout troop. Your responsibility is to coordinate the services of the troop and to build assets with the girls you serve. Part of building assets is repeatedly communicating consistent messages, messages such as "You have a lot of potential," "I care about you," "You can do this," and "You're doing this very well." Now you might be able to do a great job communicating these messages to the girls. And you might be able to hire and train staff to do the same. And if you're really good, you and your staff will "walk your talk" by behaving in a manner consistent with those messages, say, by giving the girls meaningful tasks to do, by asking their opinions, by listening to them no matter what they say.

But how many hours a day and how many days a week will you be able to be with those girls? What happens when they go home? What happens when they go to school? What happens when they shop at a store or go to a party or get a part-time job or attend a religious service? Will they hear the same messages? Will they see the same behaviors? Will they feel the same way?

Other things being equal, the more of the young person's *communities* that are on board with building assets, the more likely the young person will internalize the asset-building messages.

Here's an example of these partnerships in action. The example is from Action for Youth, a component of Tommy Tinajero and Paso del Norte Health Foundation's complex and effective asset-building efforts in El Paso, Texas:

What Young People Need, Lo Que los Jovenes Necesitan, is a project whose aim is to promote the knowledge and understanding of Search Institute's 40 developmental assets through a collaboration between Del Valle High School's English for Speakers of Other Languages (ESOL), Video Production Class, and Catholic Counseling Services, Inc. During the Summer School session and Fall Semester of 2001, students enrolled in ESOL and Video Production will receive five educational presentations on the 40 developmental assets. The parents of the ESOL students will also receive the same educational presentations.

Both parents and students will be asked to write their reflections on the presentations, and how they can apply what they learn into their daily lives. The video production students will write scripts for skits exemplifying the assets. The ESOL students will translate the scripts into Spanish. These same students and their parents will act out the scripts. The video production students will record the skits and produce a video for distribution to area shelters for battered women and nonprofit agencies working with Spanish-speaking families.

An awards banquet will be held at an area restaurant to honor the participants in the project. Each parent will receive a certificate of participation. The students will receive a certificate of participation and a T-shirt with a logo of the project.

The lessons learned from this project will be documented in reflection sheets, application sheets, and a project scrapbook. The most important aspect of this project is to educate youth and parents on the 40 developmental assets while also learning about the creative and collaborative process involved in producing an educational video.

Look at the connections in this project. First you've got a high school, and within that, two different sectors—ESOL and video production. Then you've got the faith-based counseling services. You not only bring in the parents; you involve them directly. You establish more connections with nonprofit agencies. You bring in even more of the community for the awards banquet. And you can probably bring in local businesses to donate T-shirt and logo production, facility rental, and food for the banquet. And think about the messages the young people are receiving: "You *can* learn to speak English"; "You *are* capable of producing a video"; "You *are* competent enough to translate"; "You *are* a resource to the community"; "You *can* have a home life consistent with asset building." Do you think that the same number of assets would be built were the young people merely to take a class in learning English?

Shana Overdorf, community specialist for Building Youth Assets in Raleigh, North Carolina, facilitates something similar to What Young People Need. Young people choose community-service activities in the community and a TV crew films them. The film may be just one of the highlights of periodic Family Nights; young people create and facilitate the agenda.

And in Bellevue, Washington, just across the lake from Seattle, the

Bellevue Boys and Girls Club got together with the Bellevue School District to coordinate "Project Learn." Project Learn provides the following services:

> After-school remedial educational assistance, including classes in math and reading, one-on-one homework assistance by mentors, computer access and technology skills training at the club's computer centers in public housing unit sites, and regular meetings with staff, school support service teams, and parents;

> Group recreational activities, including those involving acting, singing, dancing, arts and crafts, photography, and chess, as well as field trips to local cultural and natural attractions;

> Social skills development, including skills used to prevent drug abuse, pregnancy, and violence;

> A program that teaches young women to appreciate their bodies, develop good nutritional habits, and acquire healthy exercise habits; and

> Programs that promote interest in volunteerism and community service.

Some of the assets built by Project Learn are Positive adult relationships, Community values youth, Youth as resources, Service to others, Safety, Achievement motivation, Homework, School engagement, Bonding to school, Equality and social justice, Responsibility, Restraint, Cultural competence, Resistance skills, Peaceful conflict resolution, and Self-esteem. But again, think of all the different places and all the different activities in which students receive those same strength-based messages. This can happen only through coordinating activities in a variety of organizations that affect a young person's life.

The Cornerstone Project, in San Jose, California, takes this one step further. It coordinates a web of about 100 organizations throughout the Santa Clara Valley in an effort to infuse the asset framework into systems and programs; it acts as a source of information, training, and support for individuals and organizations interested in learning about and building assets. For example, the project worked with the City of San Jose to integrate assets into its RFP (Request for Proposals) process. The Cornerstone Project designed an "outreach listening team" to Vietnamese, Hispanic, and gay/lesbian/transgender communities, and conducted focus groups to determine how assets were built in those communities. They're currently conducting similar focus groups with Filipino American, African American, and restorative justice communities.

Student Leadership Services, Inc., led by Pamela Voss-Page in Waterford, Michigan, builds partnerships with schools and communities. Among their many programs are Students Against Driving Drunk/Students Against Destructive Decisions (high school), Students Taking a New Direction (middle school), and Promoting Accountability and Responsibility (college). Student Leadership Services has developed a list of "Asset-Building Actions for Youth": activities that young people can lead to build assets in themselves and their peers. Each activity is associated with a number of assets. Not only that, but the list provides different venues for young people to perform these activities. Here are some examples:

### Activities in the Family

➤ Make a meal together and eat it together—weekly (primarily asset 2, but also assets 1, 11, 14, 20, 26, 30, 32, 33, 37, and 38).

➤ Discuss alcohol and other drugs with your parents (primarily asset 31, but also assets 1, 2, 6, 11, 14, 16, 28, 29, 32, 33, 37, and 38).

➤ Celebrate achievements of each family member (primarily asset 21, but also assets 1, 2, 3, 14, 16, 20, 26, 28, 37, and 38).

### Activities with Peers

➤ Write a poem about a friend and publish it in the school paper (primarily asset 33, but also assets 5, 17, 21, 24, 26, and 38).

➤ Referee or umpire at local sports games (primarily asset 18, but also assets 3, 4, 7, 8, 9, 16, 26, 30, 31, 33, 36, 37, 38, and 39).

➤ Teach peers to be assertive, confident, and say "no" to peer pressure (primarily asset 5, but also assets 8, 9, 15, 16, 18, 21, 22, 24, 26, 28, 29, 30, 31, 33, 35, 36, 37, 39, and 40).

### Activities in School

➤ Join school clubs (primarily asset 15, but also assets 3, 5, 10, 12, 14, 18, 22, 24, 26, 27, 28, 30, 31, 32, 36, 37, and 38).

➤ Find a mentor/advisor on the school staff (primarily asset 3, but also assets 5, 7, 12, 14, 16, 22, 24, 29, 31, and 33).

➤ Encourage mutual respect among peers and staff (primarily asset 12, but also assets 3, 5, 8, 9, 10, 11, 14, 15, 16, 22, and 24).

### Activities in the Community

➤ Volunteer at a nursing home (primarily asset 9, but also assets 3, 4, 7, 8, 14, 26, 28, 29, 30, 33, 34, 37, 38, and 39).

➤ Clean up a local park (primarily asset 10, but also assets 3, 4, 7, 8, 9, 13, 14, 18, 27, 30, 32, 33, 34, 38, and 39).

➤ Plan a Senior Prom for senior citizens (primarily asset 34, but also assets 3, 7, 8, 9, 14, 18, 22, 26, 30, 32, 33, 37, 38, and 39).

### Activities for the World

➤ Plant a tree (primarily asset 39, but also assets 7, 8, 9, 16, 18, 21, 22, 26, 30, 32, 33, 34, 37, 38, and 40).

➤ Organize responses to disaster relief (primarily asset 8, but also assets 1, 3, 4, 7, 9, 14, 15, 16, 18, 19, 21, 22, 24, 26, 27, 28, 30, 32, 34, 37, 38, and 39).

➤ Plan an "Empty Bowls" project to help the hungry (primarily asset 7, but also assets 1, 2, 3, 5, 8, 9, 14, 15, 16, 17, 18, 21, 22, 25, 26, 27, 28, 30, 32, 33, 34, 37, 38, and 39).

You and the young people you work with can compile similar lists, which have several benefits: They give young people an opportunity to plot their own activities. They offer a variety of ways in which young people can be resources. And they help build a continuing spiral of partnerships—between young people and their peers, young people and adults, and young people and representatives of their community.

Finally, let me return to the organization with which this section began, the San Luis Obispo County Asset Development Network, and quote again from their 2001 Jostens Our Town Award and Grant Application in which they discuss the results of the partnerships they've established. Recall that these partnerships include the 4-H, the YMCA, schools, county agencies, libraries, municipalities, and a variety of community and faith-based organizations:

*With which
community
organizations has
your organization
coordinated its
efforts?*

*To what extent
do the young people
served by your
organization get
repeated, consistent,
positive messages
from a variety of
sources in the
greater community?*

*How can you
establish more joint
activities with other
organizations?*

The Asset Development Network of San Luis Obispo County has already begun to cause institutional and policy change regarding the recognition of the value of developmental assets. The language of asset development is being incorporated into county-wide government agencies, schools, corporate grant making, community-based agencies, and organizational policies, goals, and objectives. The San Luis Obispo County Department of Social Services has included asset development as one of its operating principles. Changes such as this signal the beginning of social and institutional norm change. . . .

In another effort to change community norms, the federally funded Safe Schools/Healthy Students grant awarded to the San Luis Obispo County Office of Education included asset development activities in two of its six elements. For example, minigrant programs have begun to channel $150,000 to 48 different community-based programs to support specific asset development programming, and to institute social and institutional norm change regarding asset development for our youth.

It's efforts like this that change the norms, that will eventually make all the things we've been talking about in this book *expected*.

## Partnerships with Families

*"I want things to change around the kitchen table."*

—KEITH PATTINSON, regional director, Boys and Girls Clubs of British Columbia

What about perhaps the most important partnership—the one between your organization and young people's families? Here's more from the New Mexico Council of Camp Fire USA's *KIDS CARE Training Manual*; this part specifically addresses how staff should interact with parents:

The relationships between parents and staff in a child care program can make the difference in the success of a program. It is a vital link which is necessary for the child to develop into a caring, responsible individual. The parent/staff connection will be useful not only with disciplinary issues but also issues concerning the child's accomplishments and development. In order to develop good working relationships with parents, staff should follow these guidelines:

- ➤ Always introduce themselves to new parents or family members in the program.
- ➤ Share information with parents on a regular basis.
- ➤ Provide some type of orientation for parents new to the program.
- ➤ Greet parents every time they arrive or depart from the program.
- ➤ Greet parents by name and use friendly voices, expressions, and gestures.
- ➤ Hold regular parent events.
- ➤ Invite parents to share their talents with the children.
- ➤ Maintain a Parent Information Center.
- ➤ Show interest in each family's lives and show respect to all without bias.
- ➤ Recognize that some cultures like direct communication while others prefer indirect.
- ➤ Staff should never discuss confidential material in front of children or other adults.
- ➤ Family members should know where the parent center is located and should be able to find their children's belongings easily.
- ➤ Conversations with family members should not take the attention away from children or their activities.

Think in terms of assets: Family support, Positive family communication, Caring school (club) climate, Parent involvement in (club activities) schooling. And think also in terms of numbers: Combining before- and after-school care at 24 different sites, the New Mexico Council of Camp Fire USA serves 1,000 5- to 11-year-old children each and every day. That's a lot of messages being communicated and reinforced.

Camp Fire USA provides a "Family Take-Home Page" as part of its various projects. Here's one example:

Camp Fire USA projects help build caring, confident youth and future leaders.

*All About Me* is a project on the Trail to Knowing Me that helps children to develop healthy self-images and explore peer relationships. As a result of the project:

➤ Children learn different ways to handle conflict.

➤ Children recognize personal qualities and accomplishments.

➤ Children learn to appreciate differences and develop a healthy self-image.

➤ Children experience how it feels to help someone else.

This project supports Camp Fire USA outcomes. We hope that your child:

➤ Expresses feelings and emotions in a positive, constructive manner.

➤ Is aware of personal values.

➤ Acts in a way that respects differences.

➤ Is able to leave potentially violent or dangerous situations.

➤ Is aware of others and their needs.

In addition, the project reinforces language arts, mathematics, science, and behavioral studies educational standards. For more information about these standards, contact your child's group leader.

**At Home:**

I Can Handle Conflict!

The children acted out conflict situations using the following conflict "cool-down" techniques:

➤ Always think about the problem, not the person.

➤ Stay calm.

➤ Always listen.

➤ Never use threats or name-calling.

➤ Use friendly words.

➤ Talk about fears and frustrations.

➤ Take a deep breath and count to 10 to cool off.

Help your child practice and learn more about conflict by completing the *I Can Handle Conflict* activity sheet. Use the conflict "cool-downs" listed.

This "Family Take-Home Page" contains all the components that you might want to consider for your own take-home pages. It describes to parents what their children are doing. It gives parents a "big picture" of how these activities relate to important goals. And it gives parents something to do to reinforce what they've learned.

Christy Brandenstein, the senior program director at the Y-CAP YMCA in Nashville, uses a variety of strategies to build assets with her young charges. In the Legacy Program, 10 girls of single-mother families talk about their missing parent, as do the 10 mothers; each pair then comes together to draw a Coat of Arms and discuss family goals. In the Junior Counselor Program, 13- and 14-year-old children are trained in supervision and conflict resolution and then assume some of the responsibilities of staff members.

You can do more asset building with families than just involving them in activities. Heidi Struve-Harvey, the community outreach specialist from Washoe County, Nevada, coordinated the Sandra Neese Mentoring Program, which was recently taken over by Big Brothers Big Sisters of America because they could recruit more mentors. As part of the mentoring program, they required a two-hour orientation for parents and prospective mentees; parents and their children would complete a checklist, determine ways to spend more meaningful time together, select a few assets to work on, and build an action plan for each asset using these instructions:

1. Write a brief scenario where this asset has not been present.
2. In order to start building this asset, I need my parent/guardian to:
   In order to start building this asset, I need to:
3. We will start building this asset on (day, date) at (time). This asset needs to be worked on each (day or scenario) at (time, if applicable). This asset will need to be worked on in/at (location).
4. My parent/guardian can support me in building this asset by:
   I can support my parent/guardian in building this asset by:
5. My parent/guardian and I will discuss progress on this asset (day, date) in/at (location) at (time). If things are going well, my parent/guardian and I will celebrate by:
   If things are not going well, my parent/guardian and I will:
6. We will meet with program staff to discuss progress on our asset building on (day, date) at (location) at (time).

In Struve-Harvey's Court Diversion Program, first-time felons participate in similar activities. One evening focuses on an orientation to juvenile law, and the other focuses on assets. The teenagers write on one sheet of paper what they were arrested for; next, they write on a second sheet of paper an alternative scenario of how the situation can play out more positively the next time; then they throw out the first sheet of paper.

The little things make the difference. For example, when parents and their children introduce each other in this program, they begin with the phrase, "This is _____, and the best thing about _____ is _____." Again, like so many activities in this book, this one is portable. You can use it virtually anywhere and anytime you want people to introduce each other. You can probably use it when people introduce *themselves*, too: "My name is _____, and the best thing about me is _____." In fact, that's what Stephanie Hoy, director of training and community services at Assets for Colorado Youth, does in trainings: She has participants write cards with assets on them and then personalize them. People introduce themselves by saying their name and then describing how they work on a particular asset.

It's a basic communication strategy to be sensitive to the diversity, as well as the experiences, of your audience. For example, many adults—for one reason or another—have had unpleasant experiences in schools, so consider that when you're inviting parents to meet in a school. Transportation and child care are also issues. Kit Kryger, program director at the Christie School, talked about the school's efforts to hold a family night on the first and third Wednesdays of every month. Marylhurst is about 20 miles from Portland, and the school sent out vans, provided child care, and offered dinner, in addition to facilitating the support groups and other activities; it even changed the dinner time to accommodate more parents. And Jenifer Gauthier, of the YMCA of Greater Seattle, says that with a culturally diverse population, it's crucial for the Y to present materials with content and in a manner consistent with those cultures. So as a matter of course they facilitate focus groups with different communities—and they translate their materials whenever they can. At least two things are accomplished by this effort: People from a variety of cultures get important information; and people from a variety of cultures get the important message that the YMCA cares enough about them to find out what they need.

How do you really know if the messages you want to espouse are being faithfully communicated outside your organization? One set of tools comes from the Columbia Villa/Tamarack Community, which I alluded to earlier in conjunction with Janus Youth Programs. Here are questions from three surveys that Tillie MakePeace uses to gather information from parents about neighborhoods, schools, and homes:

### Neighborhood Information

1. The things I enjoy about my community are . . .
2. The kinds of help that are available for my family and me are . . .
3. The educational and recreational activities that my family and I enjoy in the community are . . .

[Response options for the following questions are never, once a year, monthly, weekly, daily.]

Someone in the community praises my child . . .

My child helps someone in the community . . .

My child visits other families in our neighborhood . . .

My whole family participates in a community activity . . .

### School Information

1. Some things that I want the school to do better for my child are . . .
2. What I want my child to learn at school is . . .
3. The way that my child's teacher and I work together is . . .

[Response options for the following questions are never, once a year, monthly, weekly, daily.]

I help my child do his/her homework . . .

I receive communication from my child's school . . .

My child has friends join him/her to do homework . . .

My child takes advantage of tutor/mentor programs in the community . . .

### Home Information

1. I would like my child to behave this way at home . . .
2. The chores my child has are . . .

I reward my child by . . .

When my child doesn't do them, I . . .

3. If we had what we needed, my family would be like . . .

[Response options for the following questions are never, once a year, monthly, weekly, daily.]

I praise my child for something he/she did well . . .

I listen to my child talk about his/her experiences . . .

My family does something together at home that is fun . . .

My child plays happily with his/her brother(s)/sister(s) in the house . . .

*What is your relationship with the parents of the young people you serve?*

*How much feedback have you received from them about your services?*

*How much information have they received from you about your services?*

*How can you establish more joint activities with the parents of the young people you serve?*

Think of all the ways you can use just the neighborhood information: You can enhance the strengths of the community and try to compensate for what seems to be lacking. You can build relationships with the helping resources in the community. You can learn about how the people in the community view themselves and each other. And you can do the same with the information from schools and families.

The message for all these handouts, surveys, flyers, and the rest bears repeating: Use what works for you. Adapt. Collect only the information that you'll use and that will be helpful to you. We're not talking about standardized tests here; we're talking about ways to get information out and to bring information in. You know best what that means for your organization and the young people you serve.

*"Start slowly; go on forever."*

—RALPH HEMBRUFF, executive director,
Boys and Girls Clubs Services of Greater Victoria

# 5
# Walking You

## You and Young People

*As our children experience success in one area, whether it is in education,*

*arts, or recreation, we frequently notice a corresponding improvement*

*in the other areas of their lives. Success builds success.*

—FROM "CHRISTIE SCHOOL IS . . . CHRISTIE KIDS!"

I said at the beginning that this was your book. If you've read straight through to this point—well, here is where the real work begins. Here is where you begin—if you haven't already begun—to walk your talk. If you're serious about wanting to build assets more intentionally, not only with young people but with your family members and your friends and your colleagues as well, then you need first to check your attitudes. Remember the chart I presented in Chapter 1 that indicated the "asset richness" of your organization? Take a look at the chart again, but this time apply the attitudes to yourself.

| An Asset-Poor Individual | An Asset-Rich Individual |
| --- | --- |
| **1.** Focuses on young people's problems. | **1.** Focuses on young people's strengths. |
| **2.** Believes only certain people can build assets in young people. | **2.** Believes everyone can build assets in young people. |
| **3.** Believes young people absorb resources. | **3.** Believes young people are resources. |
| **4.** Views building developmental assets as a program. | **4.** Embraces building developmental assets as a way to interact with young people. |
| **5.** Tries primarily to affect those young people who seem to be troubled or who are troubling her or him. | **5.** Tries to affect all the young people he/she comes into contact with every day. |
| **6.** Isn't concerned with how other adults behave around young people. | **6.** Holds other adults accountable for their actions toward young people. |
| **7.** Is already building assets and is satisfied with that. | **7.** Wants to build assets more intentionally. |
| **8.** Blames others for young people's poor behavior. | **8.** Has stopped blaming others for the past and is working with others to improve the future. |

How many of the attitudes in the right-hand column do you currently hold? How many of them have you internalized to the extent that your behavior unconsciously reflects them?

Look at the chart another way—in the form of a continuum as it appears in Figure 5.1. You or anyone else in your organization can use this as a needs assessment or evaluation tool by periodically circling the number that best represents your attitude. (Hint: Higher scores are better.)

Tommy Tinajero, whom I've referred to several times in this book, once lived adjacent to a high school. On the weekends he'd been continually bothered by teenage boys making a lot of noise during lunchtime and lighting up cigarettes right by his house. He had several options, one of which was to angrily confront them and another of which was to call the police to angrily confront them. He chose a third option. He approached two of them who were being particularly obnoxious, said that he'd just bought a pizza, and invited them to have some. They agreed, and he brought the pizza over. While they were eating, he explained that he had

## Figure 5.1

# Becoming an Asset-Rich You

| 1 | 2 | 3 | 4 |
|---|---|---|---|
| I focus on young people's problems. | | | I focus on young people's strengths. |

| 1 | 2 | 3 | 4 |
|---|---|---|---|
| Only certain people can build assets in young people. | | | Everyone can build assets in young people. |

| 1 | 2 | 3 | 4 |
|---|---|---|---|
| Young people absorb resources. | | | Young people are resources. |

| 1 | 2 | 3 | 4 |
|---|---|---|---|
| Building developmental assets is a program. | | | Building developmental assets is a way to interact with young people. |

| 1 | 2 | 3 | 4 |
|---|---|---|---|
| I try to affect primarily those young people who seem to be troubled or who are troubling me. | | | I try to affect all the young people I come into contact with every day. |

| 1 | 2 | 3 | 4 |
|---|---|---|---|
| How other adults behave around young people doesn't really concern me. | | | I hold other adults accountable for their actions toward young people. |

| 1 | 2 | 3 | 4 |
|---|---|---|---|
| I'm already building assets. | | | I want to build assets more intentionally. |

| 1 | 2 | 3 | 4 |
|---|---|---|---|
| It's okay to blame others for young people's poor behavior. | | | I need to stop blaming others for the past and start working with others to improve the future. |

children of his own and he'd appreciate it if they didn't smoke around them. He was never bothered by them after that day. Tinajero chose to initiate a positive, asset-based relationship with the boys; the results were immediate and long-lasting.

So, here's the step-by-step process I recommend, particularly if you've never done this before:

1. Look over the list of the 40 developmental assets and choose one or two—just one or two—that you'd like to focus on. Choose something that's doable.

   ➤ *Let's say you choose asset 17, Creative activities, and asset 25, Reading for pleasure.*

2. Think about how you can help build those two assets with young people. Take them one at a time and think of three ways you can build each of those assets.

   ➤ *Since you work at an after-school program with 10- to 15-year-old boys and girls, maybe you could put on a play (assuming that's something that interests your young people). You could encourage the young people to brainstorm topics for the play. Some of them could write it, some of them could act in it, some of them could make props, and some of them could videotape it.*

3. Get a pen and paper, or a keyboard and monitor, and write down those strategies. Be as specific as possible; note, if you can, when you're going to use the strategy, where you're going to use it, and with whom you're going to use it.

   ➤ *You could talk with the rest of the staff at the regular Tuesday meeting. Following approval and other ideas, you could let the young people know on Wednesday and begin brainstorming topics. You could find out what everyone wants to do and begin assigning roles—writing, acting, making props, etc.—almost immediately, and think about performing the play in a month.*

4. Set a time for when you'll check on your own progress—say, in two weeks.

   ➤ *You could check on your progress in two weeks and again in another two weeks. At the first check you could determine whether everyone was involved in some creative way, and if not, why not.*

5. Keep your notes handy—in your pocket, in your purse, in your car, on your refrigerator.

> *You could keep your notes in your car; that would remind you to think about them on the way to work and on the way home.*

6. Tell at least two people what you're going to do and why you're going to do it.

> *You could tell your immediate supervisor and your coworker.*

7. Do what you planned as well and as genuinely as possible. If you run into an obstacle, don't get frustrated; think about how to get around the obstacle. Enlist the people you told to give you suggestions.

> *You could ask your supervisor for suggestions on how to enlist parents for support. You could ask your coworker about how to be sure that everyone is involved.*

8. After the two weeks—or whatever time you chose—are up, take stock. How did you do? How did you feel? What happened?

> *You could ask someone neutral to give you their opinion of how the young people in your group are handling the responsibilities. And you could ask the young people themselves how they're enjoying what they're doing.*

9. Give yourself credit for doing something positive.

> *You could tell yourself how many tools you're giving the young people—not only the concrete tools of writing, acting, building, and so on, but also the social tools of working on a team, wielding responsibility, and solving problems.*

10. Figure out how to continue focusing on the assets and maybe expanding your repertoire to other assets.

> *If the performance is successful, think about other projects you can do with the young people. For example, you could organize a reading group, in which they could read stories to local seniors, thereby focusing on asset 25, Reading for pleasure.*

I've included my recommendations in the form of a worksheet (Figure 5.2).

Make no mistake about it; you're going to run into problems. Many of the people I cite in this book—the ones who walk their talk—continually encounter obstacles:

> They can't get support from parents.
> They can't seem to reach all the young people they want to reach.
> They can't get funding for the activities they want to do.
> They can't get motivated every day with every young person.

Asset builders get over these hurdles. If they can't get support from parents, and if they've tried every way they know to enlist their support, then they find alternatives in the community—mentors, educators, community leaders, and older teenagers. If they can't seem to reach all the young people they want to reach, then they keep the doors open while still focusing on those they can reach, and they hope that the latter will be role models for the former. If they can't get funding for the activities they want to do, then they widen their search for other funding sources —to local businesses, to congregations, to universities; and if they still can't get funding, then they get together with young people to see how *they* can come up with the money, or else they find ways to do the activities with less money. And if they can't get motivated every day with every young person, then they concentrate on what they did do on those other days with those other young people.

*What will you do?*

*When will you do it?*

You don't have to do *everything*. And there are even going to be times when you get angry at the young people with whom you're supposed to be building assets. When that happens, you can do what youth worker John Linney from El Paso does: He thinks, "Be patient. He's just a kid."

## You and Adults

*"It's not a light switch you can flick and everybody immediately gets it."*

—NEIL NICOLL, president and CEO, YMCA of Greater Seattle

If you're reading this, you're probably connected in some way with an organization that serves youth. You may also have a spouse or partner, as well as friends and other relatives and acquaintances. As such, you have opportunities to influence all those adults.

I discussed at some length how, depending on your role in your organization, you can affect how that organization relates to young people. Here's a brief summary:

➤ You can strive to form and maintain genuine relationships with young people that are characterized by an equality of power and control.

➤ You can seek out mentors for young people.

➤ You can give youth a greater say in their lives, particularly in how they're affected by the activities facilitated in the organization.

- ➤ You can facilitate activities for both individuals and small groups that give young people opportunities to act as resources and to build their own assets.
- ➤ You can form a vision of an asset-rich environment—friendly, supportive, and respectful of youth. You can then communicate that vision to as many people as you can—continually.
- ➤ You can help translate that vision into a mission and philosophy that govern the policies of your organization and how people within the organization behave.
- ➤ You can help to set goals consistent with the vision, mission, and philosophy of the organization.
- ➤ You can see to it that all adults in the organization—administrators, staff, part-time workers, volunteer workers at every level—are trained in the developmental assets framework.
- ➤ You can reach out to form partnerships with the other institutions in young people's lives—businesses, media, schools, congregations, law enforcement, and social services.
- ➤ You can regularly gather information to assess how well the organization is building assets.

That's how you can affect youth. But you can also affect adults by doing these same things:

- ➤ You can help change other adults' lives by encouraging them to become involved in positive relationships with young people.
- ➤ You can show mentors how their own outlooks have changed as a result of their relationship with youth.
- ➤ You can point out to adults how capable and responsible youth can be if given the chance, for example, to sit on decision-making boards or to form their own councils.
- ➤ You can help adults see your vision and thus strive for something positive rather than always trying to fix something negative.
- ➤ You can adopt a personal mission and philosophy that act as models for other adults in your life.
- ➤ You can work with your colleagues to direct the organization to asset-building activities.

- ➤ You can make adults aware of the individual assets they in turn can help build with young people.
- ➤ You can help change the norms of the community by involving as many institutions as possible in communicating the asset message.
- ➤ You can collect stories of how young people have excelled in asset-rich environments and use those stories when talking with city officials, funders, or parents about what young people can do.
- ➤ You can watch your community and the people who live in it prosper from the efforts of youth.

I hope you use the charts, lists, surveys, and tools I've offered in this book. But in the end, this is not about charts, lists, surveys, and tools. It's about calling young people by their names, asking them for their opinions, listening to what they have to say, making an effort to see things from their perspective, and advocating for them in your community. We've all been young, and we all deserve a chance to participate in our own future.

*What will you do?*

*When will you do it?*

We can talk about developmental assets all day and night, but it's when we *walk* our talk that good things really start to happen.

**Figure 5.2**

# Step-by-Step Asset Building

1. Choose one or two assets to focus on.

   Asset: _____

   Asset: _____

2. Think of three ways in which you can help build each of those assets with young people.

   Asset: _____

   • _____

   • _____

   • _____

   Asset: _____

   • _____

   • _____

   • _____

3. Write down the specific strategies.

| Strategy | When to Use It | Where to Use It | With Whom to Use It |
|----------|----------------|-----------------|---------------------|
| _____ | _____ | _____ | _____ |
| _____ | _____ | _____ | _____ |
| _____ | _____ | _____ | _____ |
| _____ | _____ | _____ | _____ |
| _____ | _____ | _____ | _____ |
| _____ | _____ | _____ | _____ |
| _____ | _____ | _____ | _____ |
| _____ | _____ | _____ | _____ |

4. When will you check on your progress? _____

5. Where will you keep your notes? _____

6. Whom will you tell what you're going to do and why you're going to do it? _____

   _____

   _____

   _____

   _____

**7.** Identify obstacles and address them.

| Obstacle | Possible Solution | Source of Help |
|---|---|---|
| _____ | _____ | _____ |
| _____ | _____ | _____ |
| _____ | _____ | _____ |
| _____ | _____ | _____ |
| _____ | _____ | _____ |
| _____ | _____ | _____ |
| _____ | _____ | _____ |
| _____ | _____ | _____ |

**8.** After you check on your progress:

How did you do? _____

_____

_____

How did you feel? _____

_____

_____

What happened? _____

_____

_____

**9.** How will you reward yourself for doing something positive? _____

_____

_____

_____

_____

**10.** How will you continue to focus on the assets and maybe expand your repertoire to other

assets?_____

_____

_____

_____

_____

# Your Questions

Here are the questions I posed after each section of the book. Think about these. Discuss them with administrators, staff, and young people in your organization. And determine what to do as a result of your responses.

## 1. Your Book

**Missions**

➤ What is your personal mission?

➤ What is your organization's mission?

➤ Are you committed to making a positive difference in the lives of young people?

➤ What, specifically, are you committed to doing?

**Developmental Assets**

➤ Which assets do you think the young people you know need most?

➤ Which assets do you feel most comfortable in helping young people build?

**Asset Builders**

➤ Which people around you—adults and young people—are "natural" asset builders?

➤ How could you enlist them to be more intentional with their efforts?

## 2. Walking Relationships

### What Young People Want

➤ Have you asked young people what they want from your organization?

➤ Have you asked them what they have to offer your organization?

➤ Have you given them the opportunity to provide you with feedback on what you've been doing?

➤ Do you really listen to them?

### Changing the Rules

➤ What rules guide the relationships between the adults and young people in your organization?

➤ Do the rules need to change?

➤ How would that happen?

### Mentoring

➤ What kinds of mentoring—formal or informal—exist in your organization?

➤ Who needs mentoring?

➤ Who would make the best mentors?

➤ Do you think of yourself as a mentor?

➤ What would change if you did?

## 3. Walking Environments

### The Youth Card

➤ How do you involve youth in your organization?

➤ How do you *meaningfully* involve youth in your organization?

➤ How do your acceptance of the asset framework and your desire to help youth build assets square with your attitudes about individual young people?

➤ Are you giving youth opportunities to succeed and fail?

➤ Are you giving them opportunities to rise to their potential?

### Strategies Subtle and Sublime

➤ What strategies does your organization use to provide an asset-rich environment?

➤ What boundaries exist for staff and for young people?

➤ Are they aware of these boundaries?

### Vision

➤ What is the vision of your organization?

➤ How consistent is it with the building of developmental assets?

➤ How explicit is it—can you actually visualize what you'd like to happen?

➤ How many people share this vision?

### Mission

➤ What is the mission of your organization?

➤ Does it motivate people to act in ways that are consistent with the asset framework?

### Philosophy

➤ What is the philosophy of your organization?

➤ What values does it espouse?

➤ Does it focus on strengths?

➤ Does it focus on young people?

➤ Does it focus on relationships?

### Goals and Objectives

➤ How closely are the goals and objectives of your organization tied to the organization's vision, mission, and philosophy?

➤ How closely are they tied to developmental assets?

➤ Do the objectives and activities of your organization flow directly from the goals?

➤ Are people throughout the organization clear about both the "little picture" of activities as well as the "big picture" of vision, mission, philosophy, and goals and objectives?

**Staffing**

➤ Do all the people in your organization feel that they are making a positive difference in the lives of youth?

➤ Do their job descriptions and everyday responsibilities give them the opportunities to do that?

➤ What are the criteria for hiring staff in your organization?

➤ What's important for staff to know about your organization?

➤ How are staff in your organization supported?

➤ How are staff in your organization recognized and rewarded?

**Monitoring Progress**

➤ How do you monitor what your organization is actually doing?

➤ How do you assess how well it's doing it?

➤ Are you getting systematic feedback from staff? from youth? from parents? from your community?

➤ Are you getting both qualitative and quantitative data?

➤ How do you make your assessments useful and nonthreatening?

## 4. Walking Programs and Activities

**Partnerships with Young People**

➤ Have the young people in your organization had opportunities to serve others in their community?

➤ Have you proposed projects for them that will give them tools for their future?

➤ Have you provided them with resources to help them succeed?

➤ Have they had a significant role in determining what these activities will be?

➤ Which programs and activities in your organization promote assets?

➤ Which programs and activities in your organization can you change to promote assets?

➤ Which programs and activities might you add to promote assets?

**Partnerships with Organizations**

➤ With which community organizations has your organization coordinated its efforts?

➤ To what extent do the young people served by your organization get repeated, consistent, positive messages from a variety of sources in the greater community?

➤ How can you establish more joint activities with other organizations?

### Partnerships with Families

➤ What is your relationship with the parents of the young people you serve?

➤ How much feedback have you received from them about your services?

➤ How much information have they received from you about your services?

➤ How can you establish more joint activities with the parents of the young people you serve?

## 5. Walking You

### You and Young People

➤ What will you do?

➤ When will you do it?

### You and Adults

➤ What will you do?

➤ When will you do it?

# Walkers

These are the people who shared their time, their thoughts, and their materials with me in the making of this book.

**Susan Allen**
Director, Wisconsin Positive Youth Development Initiative, Inc.
PO Box 10
Westfield, WI 53964
Phone: 608/296-9960
Fax: 608/296-9961
E-mail: wipyd@maqs.net

**Amy Anich**
Member Services Director, McGaw YMCA
1000 Grove Street
Evanston, IL 60201
Phone: 847/475-7400, x264
Fax: 847/475-7959
E-mail: amya@mcgawymca.org

**Jim Annesi**
Director of Wellness Advancement, YMCA of Metro Atlanta
100 Edgewood Avenue NE, Suite 110
Atlanta, GA 30303
Phone: 404/267-5355
Fax: 404/527-7693
E-mail: jamesa@ymcaatl.org

**Kimberlee Archie**
Family Center Coordinator, West Hill Family Enrichment Center
12704 76th Avenue S
Seattle, WA 98178
Phone: 206/772-2050
Fax: 206/772-2448
E-mail: kimberleearchie@hotmail.com

**Deanna Armstrong**
National Director of Programs, Services, and Expansion,
    Camp Fire USA
4601 Madison Avenue
Kansas City, MO 64112
Phone: 800/669-6884
Fax: 816/756-0258
E-mail: deanna.armstrong@campfireusa.org

**Jolene Beville**
Program Assistant, Edmonson County Cooperative Extension Office
227 Mammoth Cave Road
Brownsville, KY 42210-9003
Phone: 270/597-3628
Fax: 270/597-2948
E-mail: jbeville@uky.edu

**Peggy Boyd**
County Extension Agent, Wyandotte County 4-H Club
9400 State Avenue, K-State Research and Extension
Kansas City, KS 66112
Phone: 913/299-9300

Fax: 913/299-5108
E-mail: pboyd@oz.oznet.ksw.edu

**Roger Boyer**
Executive Director, Inner City Tennis
4005 Nicollet Avenue S
Minneapolis, MN 55409
Phone: 612/802-5719
Fax: 952/473-9450; Web site: www.innercitytennis.org

**Christy Brandenstein**
Senior Program Director, Y-CAP YMCA
1021 Russell Street
Nashville, TN 37206
Phone: 615/226-5577, x112
Fax: 615/226-6427
E-mail: cbrandenstein@ymcamidten.org

**Noreen Buhmann**
Site Manager, Emma B. Howe Northeast Family YMCA
2304 Jackson Street NE
Minneapolis, MN 55418
Phone: 612/789-8803
Fax: 612/789-0134
E-mail: nbuhmann@ymcampls.org

**Judy Bunnell**
former director, It's About Time for Kids
8511 15th Avenue NE
Seattle, WA 98115
Phone: 206/382-1475
Fax: 206/525-3351
E-mail: maketime@mindspring.com

**R. Delroy Calhoun**
Center Director, Bethlehem Community Center
2539 Pleasant Avenue S
Minneapolis, MN 55404

Phone: 612/872-2763
Fax: 612/872-2788
E-mail: dcalhoun@mpls.k12.mn.us

**John M. Carney**
Executive Director, Covington Family YMCA
2140 Newton Drive
Covington, GA 30014
Phone: 770/787-3908
Fax: 770/787-3909
E-mail: johnc@ymcaatlanta.org

**Cynthia Carruthers**
Associate Professor, Leisure Studies Program
University of Nevada at Las Vegas
4505 Maryland Parkway, Box 453035
Las Vegas, NV 89154-3035
Phone: 702/895-4192
Fax: 702/895-4870
E-mail: cynny@unlv.edu

**Michelee A. Curtze**
Consultant/Director, CRT/Erie City Schools
12570 Edinboro Road
Edinboro, PA 16412
Phone: 814/734-3937
Fax: 814/734-2404
E-mail: mcurtze@aol.com

**David de la Fuente**
Branch Director, High Point YMCA
3000 SW Graham
Seattle, WA 98126
Phone: 206/937-1936
Fax: 206/933-1297
E-mail: ddelafuente@hp.seattleymca.org

**The Rev. Dr. Jeanne Harvey Duncan**
611 East Lakeland Drive
PO Box 351
Allyn, WA 98524
Phone: 360/275-5652
E-zmail: revdrjhd@aol.com

**Mike Ellis**
Executive Director, Tillamook County Family YMCA
610 Stillwell Avenue
Tillamook, OR 97141
Phone: 503/842-9622
Fax: 503/815-2643
E-mail: tillamookymca@oregoncoast.com

**Richard Enfield**
4-H Youth Development Advisor
University of California Cooperative Extension
2156 Sierra Way, Suite C
San Luis Obispo, CA 93401
Phone: 805/781-5943
Fax: 805/781-4316
E-mail: rpenfield@ucdavis.edu

**Suzanne Fielding**
Executive Director, Camp Fire USA, New Mexico Council
1613 University NE
Albuquerque, NM 87102
Phone: 505/842-8787, x3019
Fax: 505/842-8777
E-mail: sfielding@campfireabq.org

**David Foster**
Youth Services Director, McGaw YMCA
1000 Grove Street
Evanston, IL 60201
Phone: 847/475-7400, x224
Fax: 847/475-7959
E-mail: davidf@mcgawymca.org

**Jenifer Gauthier**
former administrative director, YMCA of Greater Seattle
909 4th Avenue
Seattle, WA 98104
Phone: 206/382-5003
Fax: 206/382-7283
E-mail: jgauthier@seattleymca.org

**Kelly Greenwell**
Youth and Family Coordinator, West Shore Community Resources
1096 Goldstream Avenue
Victoria, BC V9B 2Y5
Canada
Phone: 250/478-1122
Fax: 250/478-9199
E-mail: kell@uvic.ca

**Nancy Gruver**
Founder, New Moon Publishing
PO Box 3620
Duluth, MN 55803
Phone: 218/728-5507
Fax: 218/728-0314
E-mail: nancyg@newmoon.org; Web site: www.newmoon.org

**Jeremy Guzman**
917 Union Street
Cary, NC 27511
Phone: 919/469-2894
Fax: 919/469-3944
E-mail: guzmanWebsites@aol.com

**Robin Haaseth**
Coordinator, It's About Time for Kids
City of Bellevue Parks and Community Services Department
PO Box 90012
Bellevue, WA 98009
Phone: 425/452-5379

Fax: 425/4527221

E-mail: rhaaseth@ci.bellevue.wa.us

**Kim Erickson Heiar**

Manager of Community Youth Development, Ridgedale YMCA

12301 Ridgedale Drive

Minnetonka, MN 55305

Phone: 952/582-8250

Fax: 952/544-4765

E-mail: kheiar@ymcampls.org

**Ralph Hembruff**

Executive Director, Boys and Girls Clubs Services of Greater Victoria

1240 Yates

Victoria, BC V8V 3N3

Canada

Phone: 250/384-9133

Fax: 250/384-9136

E-mail: hembruffr@bgcvic.org

**Alecia Hoffman**

CHESP Program Manager

Community Chest, Inc.

PO Drawer 980

Virginia City, NV 89440

Phone: 775/847-9311

Fax: 775/847-9335

E-mail: aleciakoh@aol.com

**Sissi Horton**

Site Director, John Muir Kids' Corner

Camp Fire Boys and Girls

3301 South Horton

Seattle, WA 98144

Phone: 206/461-8550

Fax: 206/535-3351

**Stephanie Hoy**

Director of Training and Community Services,
    Assets for Colorado Youth

1580 Logan Street, Suite 700

Denver, CO 80203

Phone: 303/832-1587

Fax: 303/832-3280

E-mail: stephanie@buildassets.org

**Rick Jackson**

Codirector, Center for Teacher Formation

321 High School Road NE, PMB 375

Bainbridge Island, WA 98110

Phone: 206/855-9140

Fax: 206/855-9143

E-mail: rick@teacherformation.org

**Kathy Johnson**

Executive Director, Alternatives, Inc.

2013 Cunningham Drive, #104

Hampton, VA 23666

Phone: 757/838-2330

Fax: 757/838-9215

E-mail: kjohnson@altinc.org

**David Kelly-Hedrick**

Director, Institute for Youth Service and Leadership

YMCA of Greater Seattle

909 4th Avenue

Seattle, WA 98104

Phone: 206/382-5343

Fax: 206/382-7894

E-mail: dkhedrick@mc.seattleymca.org

**Kit Kryger**

Program Director, The Christie School

PO Box 368

Marylhurst, OR 97036

Phone: 503/635-3416
Fax: 503/697-6932
E-mail: k.kryger@christieschool.org

**Tammy Lambeth**
Family Advocate, Lyon County Human Services
PO Box 1141
Silver Springs, NV 89429
Phone: 775/577-4440
Fax: 775/577-5093
E-mail: tlambeth@lyon-county.org

**Hannah Litzenburger**
Youth Page Editor, Creating Assets Reaching Youth
305 Hemlock Street
Cary, NC 27513
Phone: 919/469-3205
E-mail: hanlitz@aol.com

**Tillie MakePeace**
Program Director, Columbia Villa/Tamarack Youth Advancement Team
9029 North Dana Avenue
Portland, OR 97203
Phone: 503/283-8277
E-mail: cv@jyp.org

**Tina J. Martinez**
Director of Programs, Boys and Girls Clubs of Metro Denver
2017 West 9th Avenue
Denver, CO 80204
Phone: 303/892-9200, x122
Fax: 303/892-9210
E-mail: tinam@bgcmd.org; Web site: www.bgcmd.org

**Carol Moore**
Consultant with Staff Development, Raleigh Parks and Recreation
PO Box 590
Raleigh, NC 27602

Phone: 919/831-6640

Fax: 919/831-6470

E-mail: moore@raleigh-nc.org

**Beth Mowry**

Director of Membership, Girl Scouts—Great Valley Council

2633 Moravian Avenue

Allentown, PA 18103

Phone: 610/791-2411

Fax: 610/791-4401

E-mail: b.mowry@gs-gvc.org

**Neil Nicoll**

President and CEO, YMCA of Greater Seattle

909 4th Avenue

Seattle, WA 98104

Phone: 206/382-5004

Fax: 206/382-7283

E-mail: nnicoll@seattleymca.org

**Shana Overdorf**

Community Specialist, Building Youth Assets

626 West Jones Street

Raleigh, NC 27603

Phone: 919/755-9605

E-mail: shanaoverdorf@hotmail.com

**Cara Patrick**

Program Director, Sound Youth AmeriCorps

4759 15th Avenue NE

Seattle, WA 98105

Phone: 206/525-1213, x3201

Fax: 206/525-1218

E-mail: cpatrick@churchcouncilseattle.org

**Keith Pattinson**

Regional Director, Boys and Girls Clubs of British Columbia

7595 Victoria Drive

Vancouver, BC V5P 3Z6
Canada
Phone: 604/321-5621
Fax: 604/321-5941
E-mail: bgbc@telus.net

**William Powers**
Executive Director, The Christie School
PO Box 368
Marylhurst, OR 97036
Phone: 503/635-3416
Fax: 503/697-6932
E-mail: w.powers@christieschool.org

**Susan Ragsdale**
Trainer, YMCA of Middle Tennessee
213 McLemore Street
Nashville, TN 37203
Phone: 615/259-3418, x104
Fax: 615/255-7848
E-mail: sragsdale@ymcamidtn.org

**Julie Rehder**
Director, Success By 6, United Way of North Carolina
1413 Hattie Road
Apex, NC 27502
Phone: 919/362-4351
Fax: 919/303-1596
E-mail: jlrehder@aol.com

**Sharon Rodine**
Director, HEART of OKC Project
(Healthy, Empowered And Responsible Teens of OKC)
Oklahoma Institute for Child Advocacy
420 NW 13th Street, #101
Oklahoma City, OK 73103
Phone: 405/236-5437, x205
Fax: 405/236-1690
E-mail: srodine@oica.org

**Holly Rutherford-Allen**
Manager of Annual Giving, Girl Scouts-Mile Hi Council
400 South Broadway, PO Box 9407
Denver, CO 80209
Phone: 303/778-8774, x242
Fax: 303/733-6345
E-mail: hollyr@gsmhc.org

**Tricia Segal**
Coordinator of Young Adult Services, Fort Vancouver Regional Library
1007 East Mill Plain Boulevard
Vancouver, WA 98663
Phone: 360/759-4800
Fax: 360/693-2681
E-mail: tsegal@fvrl.org

**Ivory Smith**
Education Specialist, Boys and Girls Clubs of King County
201 19th Avenue
Seattle, WA 98122
Phone: 206/324-7317, x100
Fax: 206/324-8315
E-mail: ismith@positiveplace.org

**Terry Smith**
Recreation and Special Services Manager,
    Bellevue Parks and Recreation
City of Bellevue Parks and Community Services Department
PO Box 90012
Bellevue, WA 98009
Phone: 425/452-5379
Fax: 425/4527221
E-mail: tsmith@ci.bellevue.wa.us

**Bill Stanczykiewicz**
President and CEO, Indiana Youth Institute
603 E. Washington, Suite 800
Indianapolis, IN 46204

Phone: 317/396-2710
Fax: 317/396-2701
E-mail: billstan@iyi.org

**Sally Stauffer**
Recreation Coordinator, The Christie School
PO Box 368
Marylhurst, OR 97036
Phone: 503/635-3416
Fax: 503/697-6932
E-mail: s.stauffer@christieschool.org

**Heidi Struve-Harvey**
Community Outreach Specialist, Washoe County
    Department of Juvenile Services
PO Box 11130
Reno, NV 89520
Phone: 775/323-6767, x15
Fax: 775/328-3904
E-mail: hharvey@mail.co.washoe.nv.us

**Marcus Stubblefield**
Coordinator, PAAC (Promoting Assets Across Cultures) Asset Team
SafeFutures Youth Center
6337 35th SW
Seattle, WA 98126
Phone: 206/938-9606, x107
Fax: 206/938-7540
E-mail: marcuss@sfyc.net

**Amy Swisher**
Communications Coordinator, First Day Foundation
210 Main Street, PO Box 10
Bennington, VT 05201
Phone: 877/FIRSTDAY
Fax: 802/447-9670
E-mail: firstday@sover.net

**Noella Tabladillo**
Communications Director, The Cornerstone Project
1922 The Alameda
San Jose, CA 95126
Phone: 408/351-6482
Fax: 408/298-0143
E-mail: www.projectcornerstone.org

**Sharon Tebbutt**
113 Hedgerow Court
Cary, NC 27513
Phone: 919/462-8172
E-mail: Sharon_tebbutt@ncsu.edu

**Tommy Tinajero**
former program officer,
    Paso del Norte Health Foundation
1100 North Stanton, Suite 520
El Paso, TX 79902
Phone: 915/544-7636
Fax: 915/544-7713

**Peter Tompkins-Rosenblatt**
Program Director, Janus Youth Programs, Inc.
707 NE Couch
Portland, OR 97232
Phone: 503/233-6090, x4275
Fax: 503/233-6093
E-mail: prosenblatt@starband.net

**Melissa Bachman Ugland**
former coordinator, Mosaic Youth Center
7323 58th Avenue N
Crystal, MN 55428
612/749-9561
E-mail: info@mosaicyouthcenter.com

**Karen VanderVen**
Professor
Department of Psychology in Education
University of Pittsburgh
Pittsburgh, PA 15260
Phone: 412/524-6945
E-mail: kvander@pitt.edu

**Gail Vessels**
Vice President of Organizational Effectiveness,
    Boys and Girls Clubs of Greater Kansas City
6301 Rockhill Road, Suite 303
Kansas City, MO 64131
Phone: 816/361-3600
Fax: 816/361-3675
E-mail: gvessels@bgc-gkc.org

**Paul Vidas**
Director, United with Youth
United Way Fox Cities
1820 Appleton Road
Menasha, WI 54952
Phone: 920/954-7210
Fax: 920/954-7209
E-mail: paul.vidas@unitedway.org

**Pamela Voss-Page**
Executive Director, Student Leadership Services, Inc.
1200 West Huron, Suite 206
Waterford, MI 48328
Phone: 248/706-0757
Fax: 248/706-0750
E-mail: pgvp@sadd.org

**Bette Wahl**
Project Coordinator, Eau Claire Coalition for Youth
PO Box 496
Eau Claire, WI 54702-0496

Phone: 715/839-1681

E-mail: bette.wahl@ci.eau-claire.wi.us

**Carol White**

School-Age Child Care Director, Tillamook County Family YMCA

610 Stillwell Avenue

Tillamook, OR 97141

Phone: 503/842-9622

Fax: 503/815-2643

E-mail: tillamookymca@oregoncoast.com

**Alfonso Wyatt**

Vice President, Fund for the City of New York

121 6th Avenue

New York, NY 10013

Phone: 212/925-6675

Fax: 212/925-5675

E-mail: awyatt@fcny.org

Young people from Seattle Youth Employment Program, Seattle, Washington:

> **Brittany Carter**
> **April Lorenzo**
> **LaCale Pringle**
> **Victoria Tangata**

Young people from Paso del Norte Health Foundation, El Paso, Texas:

> **Crystal Espinoza**
> **Elisa Macias**
> **Pamela Marquez**
> **Juanita McCray**
> **Barnabie Mejia**
> **Emmanuel Ortega**
> **Israel Rivera**
> **Alexandra Rodriguez**
> **Viridiana Rodriguez**
> **Barbara Silva**

Young people from Y-Leaders in Training, Victoria, British Columbia:
**Julie Boulet**
**Jenna MacLeod**
**Leonard Steen**
**Tanya Tosczak**

All the young people from the High Point Asset Team,
Seattle, Washington

All the young people and staff from the Christie School,
Marylhurst, Oregon

All the other young people and adults who talked to me about their
lives and assets everywhere I visited

# Index

## About the Author

Neal Starkman has been a curriculum developer since the mid-1970s. He has helped develop numerous materials in the field of health education, including comprehensive curricula in drug education, HIV/AIDS prevention, violence prevention, and peer helping. In addition, he has written or produced books, videotapes, audiotapes, plays, songs, posters, learning games, and simulations on a variety of topics. He has also designed training workshops and marketing materials. Starkman's other books relating to developmental assets are *Ideas That Cook: Activities for Asset Builders in Schools* and *Great Places to Learn: How Asset-Building Schools Help Students Succeed*, the latter of which was cowritten with Peter Scales and Clay Roberts.

Starkman holds a Ph.D. in social psychology from the University of Connecticut (1975); he is the owner of a company called Flashpoint Development, which specializes in innovative health education. Before his son, Cole, was born in 1995, he had time and energy to write two novels and publish fiction, nonfiction, and academic papers in national magazines and journals. He lives in Seattle.